GOD & SEX Marriage

GUIDANCE FROM 1 CORINTHIANS 7

A piece of writing is never finished; it is merely abandoned.

GOD
SEX
& Marriage

GUIDANCE FROM 1 CORINTHIANS 7

JOHN RICHARDSON

Cartoons by Taffy Davies

MPA Books - Biblical Application Series
God, Sex and Marriage: Guidance from 1 Corinthians 7
John P. Richardson
Copyright © John Richardson, 1995, 1998

Published in the United Kingdom by
The Good Book Company
Elm House, 37 Elm Road, New Malden, Surrey KT3 3HB
Tel: 0845 225 0880; Fax: 0845 225 0990
email: admin@thegoodbook.co.uk ; website: www.thegoodbook.co.uk

ISBN 1 873166 70 2

Published in Australia by
MPA Books, 9, Cudgee Close, Baulkham Hills, NSW 2153

National Library of Australia
Cataloguing in Publication Data
ISBN 0 646 22487 5

Designed by Kevin Wade
Cover Design by Tim Thornborough
Illustrations © Taffy Davies 1995
Printed in China

Contents

Introduction

NOT ANOTHER BOOK ON MARRIAGE!

When I told one person I was working on a book about marriage her response was to wonder why I was writing about a subject on which there was so much material already. 'Why not,' she asked, 'write about the ways in which God has encouraged you as a single person?' One reason is that often I *haven't* felt particularly encouraged by being single! But a second reason (not unrelated to the first) is that whilst there are many books which contain good *advice* on the subject of marriage, there seem to be very few which contain good *theology*. So, **this book aims to show how principles for courtship and marriage can be found in the Bible**.

This also helps answer a second question which might arise: 'What is a single man doing writing a book about *marriage?*' The answer is that this is not a book about *my* views on marriage; it is a book about what the Bible has to say. It is worth pointing out that the apostle Paul and Jesus himself were also single men. The doctrine of the *inspiration* of the Bible assumes that the Holy Spirit is not limited in what he can say by the human material he uses. And in any case, the best view of the game is not always from the pitch. However, I've had my share of relationships and experiences, which were another reason why this book came to be written. Uncomfortable about the way some of these had gone, I began looking through the Bible to find out what I had been doing wrong. In the course of this I realized that 1 Corinthians 7 contained everything I needed to know provided I read it properly.

The book that most helped me do so was Gordon Fee's commentary on *The First Epistle to the Corinthians* (Grand Rapids: W.B. Eerdmans, 1987). Where I have referred to 'Fee' in the text I mean this commentary. It is a great book, but unfortunately it is also a very big, technical and expensive book and not the sort of thing you are likely to read unless you have a knowledge of Greek and a lot of time on your hands. This brings me to another reason for writing, which is **to bring you some of the insights of the best scholars in a cheap and readable format**.

Of course, these scholars don't always agree with one another – or with me! Sometimes I have taken one side in a translational or theological dispute where other options are available, but I don't always go into all the details where the arguments are beyond the scope of this book. Where this is the case, however, I have usually given page references in Fee which the interested reader can pursue.

In addition to Fee, I have referred to a large number of other works both on 1 Corinthians and on sex and marriage – too many to list. The ones to which I have *specifically* referred in the text are given in the endnotes. The curious may want to check these, the trusting will take my word for it.

However, I would also recommend the following two books which aren't in the endnotes:

Clifford & Joyce Penner	*The Gift of Sex* and *A Gift for all Ages* (Milton Keynes: Word UK Ltd.) for good advice and theology on sexual matters.
Anne Atkins	*Split Image* (London, Hodder & Stoughton, 1987) hard to obtain, but one of the most helpful books I've read on gender issues.

BIBLE VERSIONS AND REFERENCES
Various Bible translations have been referred to in this book, for which the abbreviations are as follows:

GNB	Good News Bible
KJV	King James Version, also known as the Authorized Version
NASB	New American Standard Bible
NEB	New English Bible
NIV	New International Version
RSV	Revised Standard Version

Bible references are by book, chapter and verse, using standard abbreviations, e.g. 'Eze 16:8' is a reference to Ezekiel, chapter 16, verse 8. 'Cf.' means 'compare', i.e. 'you might find it useful to look this up'.

TECHNICALITIES

The Greek text used was the Nestlé-Aland 26th Edition (Copyright 1966, 1968, 1975, 1983 by the United Bible Societies). The Bible software was Logos 1.6b (Copyright Logos Research Systems Inc. 1991-93). The coffee was percolated and the tea was mostly Earl Grey. Where I have not used my own translation I have generally quoted from the RSV. Most people, I am sure, will be using the NIV, but I still find the RSV better (if less readable) and I certainly think the NIV reader should also have reference to the RSV, NASB or KJV for study purposes.

Some people may object to the RSV's 'sexist' language – and my own retention of terms like the generic 'men' in translation. What I would *like* to say on this subject would fill another book. But let me simply state that attempts to use 'inclusive' language are increasingly denying the 'non-inclusive' nature of the original Biblical text. The Greek *anthrōpos*, for example, can be translated 'a person' but it is derived from *anēr*, meaning 'a man', and whilst it can indicate a *particular* man (e.g. in 1 Corinthians 7:1), it is never to my knowledge used in this way for a woman. The argument that Greek is more 'inclusive' than English does not hold much water and we are in danger of lying about Scripture in an attempt to make it more palatable. Personally, I prefer to stick to the text and confront the offence.

ACKNOWLEDGEMENTS

I am grateful to those people who have consciously or unconsciously kept me going with this project. I am especially grateful to those who read through various versions of the text and helped me make it more intelligible to the general reader. Thanks are also due to Taffy Davies for the excellent cartoons.

John P. Richardson
January 1995

Chapter 1

The Corinthian Background

WHAT WAS THE QUESTION?

The answer is 1 Corinthians 7. Now what was the question? This is the problem that faces us as we begin unravelling this part of the Bible. It is obvious from the first verse – 'Now concerning *the things about which you wrote…*' – that Paul is answering a letter the Corinthians had sent to him. If only we had this letter life would be so much easier! Much of what we deduce from 1 Corinthians 7, as with other parts of the Bible, will depend on what we think were the questions behind the text. Working these out is sometimes straightforward, sometimes more difficult, and a lot of this book is taken up with this issue.

And here we must sidetrack for a moment. One of the biggest questions facing Christians today is 'How can we understand the Bible properly?' In particular, what do we do when *alternative* understandings of the same Bible passage are on offer? Of course, everyone will agree we should pray about it, but some Christians (mistakenly) feel this is enough. They believe that God will 'just reveal' the right answer to them 'through his Spirit' and that they will know what this is 'instinctively'. But though this sounds fine, it ignores the nature of the Bible itself. The Bible is a *book*, and the way to understand a book is the same whether it is the Bible or the book you are now holding. The right understanding is *the one that makes best sense of the text*, not the one that agrees with your opinions or intuitions. God would not have revealed himself to us through a *book* if he had intended us to understand him in another way not related to books. When we pray, therefore, it should be that God will help us use the available resources *properly* to come to a right understanding of the Bible. It should not be that God will save us the effort by giving us a vision or an intuition that makes the hard work unnecessary!

So to know what the questions are that 1 Corinthians 7 sets

out to answer we will often have to do some detective work. The inexperienced reader may perhaps feel this is unnecessarily complex, but we must do it *and it is worth the effort*! Once we know the questions, the value of the answers becomes obvious. *Until* we know them, the answers may be positively dangerous! As we will see, 1 Corinthians 7 may be a minefield for the unwary, but it is a gold-mine for the diligent.

THE BACKGROUND

Our story begins around 50AD when the Apostle Paul visited the Greek town of Corinth (see Acts 18). Along with a married couple called Priscilla and Aquila, and joined later by his fellow missionaries Silas and Timothy, Paul established a church there. Due to the fruitful nature of the work (Acts 18:9-10) Paul stayed over eighteen months before he left for Syria, taking Priscilla and Aquila with him. Yet for all his hard work, the church at Corinth seems to have caused Paul more headaches than all the others put together. Only two years later he is having to write the first of the two letters to the Corinthians contained in the Bible, and from 1 Corinthians 5:9 we know there was at least one more of which we have no other record. Both the Biblical letters are full of rebuke and warning from the Apostle and reveal an alarming situation in the Corinthian church. Immorality, immaturity and unfaithfulness abound. The members are divided amongst themselves and alienated from the Apostle. They are proud where they should be humble and weak where they should be strong. In fact, when you read Paul's letters, it is amazing that any modern church would want to model itself on that at Corinth, even though so many apparently do!

THE PROBLEM WITH SEX

One of the biggest problem areas for the Corinthians was sexuality (so at least in this respect little has changed today). Chapters 5 and 6 reveal an appalling catalogue of sins, including incest and prostitution! Yet the church was apparently blind to these – they are not included in the things 'about which' they wrote to Paul. The Apostle must have been in despair! Yet we can be thankful that because the Corinthians so soon departed from the ways of the Gospel we have the benefit of Apostolic teaching on issues that would inevitably have arisen one day.

You would do well to read through the earlier chapters of 1 Corinthians for yourself and think about the principles of Christian behaviour they contain. Notice in particular how Paul roots his teaching about Christian living in the Old Testament and the basic principles of the Gospel. His teaching on sexuality goes right back to Genesis 2:24 (see 6:16), yet all the time that he is criticizing the Corinthians he is also affirming their true liberty in Christ.

However, in this book we must concentrate on chapter 7. This is partly for reasons of space, but mainly because in its forty densely-packed verses this chapter has something for everyone, whether married, widowed, separated, single or courting. A careful reading of these verses will not only help you understand your own situation better but may prepare you for change, whether it be the sorrows of bereavement or the joys of marriage. It would be no exaggeration to describe 1 Corinthians 7 as God's 'Marriage Guidance'. I hope a prayerful reading of it, and the suggestions contained in this book, help you understand what that is.

Chapter 2

Sex and Marriage

1 Corinthians 7:1-6

[1]Now concerning the things about which you wrote: it is good for a man not to touch a woman – [2]but because of sexual immoralities, let every husband go on having his own wife, and let every wife go on having her own husband. [3]The husband should render to his wife what is her due, and likewise also the wife to her husband. [4]The wife does not have authority over her own body but the husband does, and likewise also the husband does not have authority over his own body but the wife does. [5]Do not deprive one another, except perhaps by agreement for a time, that you might give yourselves to prayer. And then come together again, that Satan might not tempt you through your lack of self-control. [6]But this I say as a concession, not as a command.

A WARNING TO THE FAINT-HEARTED!

This book is rather like a tadpole – the head (this chapter) is a good deal bigger than the tail (the other chapters of the book). You may find this chapter hard going because our understanding of 1 Corinthians 7 depends on the meaning of the first paragraph, and this in turn depends on the meaning of the very first sentence. We have to spend some time examining the language and logic of these opening words to prepare us for the rest of 1 Corinthians 7.

Basically there are three questions to be answered:

1. Is Paul addressing single people or someone else?
2. Is Paul talking about marriage or something else?
3. Does v.1 express Paul's own opinion or someone else's?

Most English translations of the Bible, most commentaries and most teaching on this passage seem to assume the first option in each case. However, I will to try to show that the second option in fact makes better sense.

I will argue that the first paragraph of 1 Corinthians 7 is addressed to married people, not the single, that it is concerned with sexual relations within marriage, not marriage itself, and that v.1 expresses the opinion of one section of the Corinthian church, with which Paul disagrees.

If you are happy to take my word for all this you can skip straight to the 'Summary' at the end of this chapter. However, if you want your money's worth I suggest you read on, or at least come back to this at a later stage. (You will probably need to do so anyway, the first time you find you disagree with my position!)

THE NATURE OF MARRIAGE
First, then, I would want to suggest that the opening paragraph of 1 Corinthians 7 is about *sex within marriage*. This may not be obvious from whatever translation of the Bible you are using, so we will have to spend a little while proving the point. Don't think this is a waste of space – it is very important that we know what the passage is about before we start applying it. And if you are unmarried don't be tempted to think this chapter isn't relevant to you. On the contrary – you should read it particularly carefully! If you know what marriage is about you will know what you are letting yourself in for by getting married. You may even decide you are not ready for it yet!

THE PROBLEM OF INTERPRETATION

Because of the problems with interpreting 1 Corinthians 7, the translation at the beginning of each chapter of this book is my own. Most English translations (e.g. NIV, GNB, etc.) seem to share the assumption that the Corinthians had asked Paul about *marriage* and they give the unfortunate impression that Paul was basically against it. My own translation, by contrast, talks about husbands and wives from v.2 onwards because I think that the Corinthians' question concerned *sex* and that, within marriage, Paul was basically for it.

Reading most modern translations, this opening paragraph seems to suggest that those who cannot live the single life should get married. This understanding is also implied by the words of the old *Book of Common Prayer* marriage service, which says that marriage was given 'that such persons as have not the gift of continency [i.e. self-control] might ... keep themselves undefiled members of Christ's body'. Marriage, according to this view, is for those who can't control themselves!

But this understanding creates a number of problems. In Genesis 2:18 God says, 'It is *not good* that the man should be alone', and then goes on to create a woman to be his wife. Surely Paul is not saying this was just a concession to Adam's weakness? Indeed he is not, for he wrote at a later stage that those who forbade marriage were teaching 'doctrines of demons' (1 Timothy 4:1-3). Even in 1 Corinthians 7 itself Paul seems to be in favour of marriage. In 7:9 he says that certain widows should marry, in 7:27 he says it is not a sin to marry and in 7:36 he suggests some couples definitely should marry. But we needn't look so far ahead. If v.1 means Paul is against marriage, he contradicts himself in v.2. It is easy to see this when we look at a translation like the NIV and the apparent assumptions underlying it:

1 Corinthians 7:1-2 (NIV)	Assumptions
¹Now for the matters you wrote about:	Paul begins to answer the Corinthians' letter, and though he does not tell us what they said...
It is good for a man not to marry.	he gives his own opinion (or at least agrees with theirs) that *it is good not to marry.*
²But because there is so much immorality, each man should have his own wife, and each woman her own husband.	However, life being the way it is, *people ought to marry!*

On this reading Paul is made to say (a) singleness is good and
(b) marriage is necessary – which presents us with an impossible
dilemma! And notice he does not say '*some* people *may* marry' but
'*each* man *should* have his own wife, etc.' Put like this, marriage is
a command for all! To remain single would be disobedient (even
though according to v.1 it would be a good thing!)

By this stage we may despair of making any sense of the
passage and go on to read something else. However, if we are
prepared to examine the passage carefully in its context and
compare it with other parts of the Bible we will find that there is
an alternative understanding which makes sense not only of the
opening paragraph but of the whole chapter.

SEX IS THE SUBJECT
As indicated at the beginning of this chapter, v.1 of 1 Corinthians
7 should be translated literally: 'it is good for a man not to *touch* a
woman'. *But this literal translation cannot be taken literally!* No one
has ever imagined that the Apostle meant men should avoid any
physical contact with women (though the NEB – 'It is a good
thing for a man to have nothing to do with women' – runs pretty
close.) To get round this the NIV, along with many modern
Christians, assumes that 'touch' means 'marry' – but we have
seen the problems this causes.

A better explanation, consistent with both the original Greek
and the rest of the chapter, is that *Paul is talking not about marriage
but about sex*. In the first place, the usual Greek expression for
marrying is 'to take' a wife. The expression 'to touch', used here,
appears elsewhere in the Bible as a euphemism (a polite word) for
'to have sex with'. Proverbs 6:27-29 reads:

'Can a man carry fire in his bosom and his clothes not be
    burned?
Or can one walk upon hot coals and his feet not be scorched?
So is he who goes in to his neighbour's wife;
  none who **touches** her will go unpunished.' (RSV)

In the Septuagint (the Greek translation of the Old Testament
made centuries before the birth of Jesus) the verb used here for
'touches' is exactly the same as Paul uses in 1 Corinthians 7:1.
And the meaning of the Proverb is quite clear: to 'touch' your

neighbour's wife means 'to have sexual intercourse with' her. If we accept that this is also Paul's meaning in 1 Corinthians 7:1, we could paraphrase it as follows:

'Now concerning the things about which you wrote: it is good for a man **not to have sexual relations with** a woman ...'

But why would Paul say this? To answer this question, we have to consider not only the wording but the context of the letter.

CORINTH IS THE CONTEXT

If the subject of v.1 is sex rather than marriage, does this mean (as many people quickly assume) that Paul is anti-sex, or is there another explanation for his opening words? The best answer has a long pedigree and is ingeniously simple: *Paul is simply quoting back to the Corinthians the opinion they had expressed in their earlier letter to him.* (For a full assessment of this interpretation see Fee, pp.19-20.)

Paul introduces chapter 7 with the phrase, '*Now concerning* the things about which you wrote ...' Four other times in this letter he uses the same distinctive introduction and each time he seems to be dealing with a new topic raised by the Corinthians in their letter to him:

7:25 'Now concerning the unmarried... '
8:1 'Now concerning food offered to idols... '
12:1 'Now concerning spiritual gifts...'
16:1 'Now concerning the contribution for the saints...'

Chapter 8 is especially interesting because it seems to be a clear example of what we are suggesting is happening in chapter 7. The first verse there reads:

'Now concerning food offered to idols: we know that "all of us possess knowledge." "Knowledge" puffs up, but love builds up.' (8:1, RSV)

The Corinthians' opinion in this case was that 'All of us possess knowledge.' Paul agrees with this as a statement, but disagrees with its application - we indeed possess 'knowledge', but this can lead to pride. If he is taking the same approach at the start of chapter 7, we can punctuate 7:1 in a similar way to 8:1 to indicate where Paul's words end and the Corinthians' opinion begins:

> 'Now concerning the things about which you wrote: "it is good for a man not to 'touch' a woman" ...'

But why would Paul agree with the Corinthians if he has no problem with sex? The answer probably lies partly in the problems addressed in chapters 5 and 6, and partly in the attitude to the body found in Greek philosophy.

SEX AND IMMORALITY

In 1 Corinthians as a whole, Paul does not begin to discuss the questions the Corinthians raised with him until chapter 7. He has spent chapters 5 and 6 dealing with their immorality. This same church, where a man was living with his stepmother (5:1) and others were visiting prostitutes (6:15), had not thought to ask about *these* things! Yet astonishingly it seems they *had* asked whether it was better for a man not to have sex with a woman at all. Reading the introduction to chapter 7 in the light of chapters 5 and 6, Paul's thinking probably goes something like this:

> 'Now concerning the things about which you wrote: (If you are speaking about your own immoral behaviour) "it is good for a man not to 'touch' a woman"...'

Paul's next words also suggest he is still looking back to chapters 5 and 6:

> '– but **because of sexual immoralities**, let every husband go on having his own wife, and let every wife go on having her own husband.'

Contrary to the RSV translation, Paul does not refer to 'temptation to immorality' here, as if talking about something that *might* happen, but to 'sexual immoralities' (note the plural!) in the sense of something which is happening currently. In v.1 Paul agrees that some people – specifically the immoral persons of chapters 5 and 6 – would indeed do well to avoid sexual activity altogether. The message of what follows, however, is that this definitely would not apply to everyone.

SEX AND SPIRITUALITY

We still need to ask why some people at Corinth would have regarded avoiding sexual behaviour as 'good'. The reason probably lies in what we call 'asceticism' (the 'sc' is pronounced as in 'science'). This is an understanding of spirituality which drives a wedge between physical things and spiritual things.

In asceticism the path to true spirituality lies in moving away from the things of the world in general, and physical pleasure in particular. This is achieved either by ABSTAINING from pleasure or by INFLICTING discomfort on oneself.

Though this may look peculiar in black and white, it is not hard to find examples in all the major world religions. The yogi (holy men) of Hinduism subject themselves to intense physical discipline (yoga), even to the point of bizarre or painful practices, in the hope of achieving a state of deep spirituality. Muslims fast from food, drink and sex during daylight hours throughout the month of Ramadan. Buddhists have a strong monastic tradition of poverty and simple living as a way of loosening their ties with this life. And the same attitude and similar practices have been found in Christianity. Some early Christian monks, like Simon the Stylite, used to live in the desert at the top of pillars without coming down for years. During the Middle Ages many others, including the young Martin Luther, would inflict themselves with prolonged fasting. Even today most Catholics will still give up something for Lent, whilst many Evangelicals and Charismatics hold fasts and nights of prayer.

Not surprisingly, ascetics have generally regarded something as pleasurable as sex with deep suspicion. Unfortunately, this attitude distorted Christian thinking quite early on, helped along by a theology which concluded that sexual intercourse was the physical route by which original sin was transmitted. Origen, a third century theologian, is thought to have taken Matthew 19:12 literally and castrated himself. The 'conversion' of Augustine of Hippo (386AD) was not so much to Christianity as to celibacy.[1] His problem was not whether Christ had died for his sins, but whether he could cope with giving up sex, hence his famous prayer, 'Grant me chastity and continence, but not yet.'[2]

In the Middle Ages, Yves of Chartres 'counselled the devout to abstain from sexual intercourse on Thursdays in remembrance of Christ's rapture, on Fridays in remembrance of Christ's crucifixion, on Saturdays in honour of the Virgin Mary, on Sundays in commemoration of Christ's resurrection, and on Mondays out of respect for departed souls.'[3] The devout were presumably grateful this gave them something to look forward to midweek!

Yet though we may laugh at the excesses of past ages, asceticism always impresses the person who is truly endeavouring to be spiritual. We are *all* prone, as Paul says in Colossians 2:20-21, to 'submit to regulations, "Do not handle, Do not taste, Do not touch."' The reason, as he points out, is that these practices 'have indeed an appearance of wisdom in promoting rigour of devotion and self-abasement and severity to the body' (2:23a). But Paul's condemnation of them is as scathing as it is surprising: 'they are of no value in checking the indulgence of the flesh.' (2:23b)! We see proof of this in the experience of Jerome, a fourth century monk who lived for a while as a desert hermit. He later wrote, 'Though in my fear of hell I had consigned myself to this prison where my only companions were scorpions and wild beasts, I often found myself amid bevies of girls. My face was pale, and my frame chilled with fasting; yet my mind was inflamed with desire.'[4] Jerome learnt the hard way that the more we try not to think of something, the more we think of it!

But why did Origen, Augustine, Jerome, Yves of Chartres and others have this ascetic, and particularly anti-sexual, attitude? The answer lies in a combination of Greek philosophy with a misreading of the Bible. The Greek philosophers viewed the body both with a certain suspicion and contempt, and this attitude often crept into Christian thinking. Some 400 years before Christ, Plato wrote that 'if we want to see (the soul) as it really is, we should look at it, not as we do now, when it is *deformed by its association with the body* and other evils, but in the *pure state* which reason reveals to us.'[5] For Plato, the body was basically a prison of impurity for the soul. However, what was done with the body would not *necessarily* affect the soul unless it encouraged *moral* wickedness.

It seems that the church at Corinth was influenced by this philosophy in two directions. Some – those addressed in chapter 6 – evidently felt it didn't matter what you did with your body provided it didn't directly affect your soul. Thus for them, going to prostitutes was perfectly acceptable. Others – those addressed in chapter 7 – took a rigorously ascetic line, arguing that physical pleasures such as sex would inhibit the spiritual progress of the soul. It was these people who believed that it was 'good for a man not to "touch" a woman.'

It is important to notice that Paul responds to both groups *Christianly*. He condemns the immoralities of the first group without resorting to legalism. They must give up visiting prostitutes, not because there is a 'Christian law' against it, but because they have been made to understand their new life in Christ. Yet he has no time for the asceticism of the second group, who are wrong both about sex and marriage. Even though the ascetics avoid the sin of the first group, sex and marriage are not themselves sinful.

SEX IN MARRIAGE

We need to understand that the ascetics at Corinth were against sex in *principle*. When Paul says that 'because of sexual immoralities' each man should have his own wife and each woman should have her own husband, *he is not saying that single people should get married to avoid sexual temptation.* As we have seen, the Greek expression for marrying is to 'take' a spouse. Here Paul says each man should 'have' – indeed 'go on having' – his own wife and each woman should 'go on having' her own husband. The sense is of continuing to do something they are already doing. What this is becomes clear in vv. 3-4:

'The husband should render to his wife what is her due, and likewise also the wife to her husband. The wife does not have authority over her own body but the husband does, and likewise also the husband does not have authority over his own body but the wife does.'

What is 'due' from the husband or wife to one another is the giving of their bodies. That is to say, husband and wife *owe* one another sexual satisfaction.

We need to be particularly careful to understand what this means for the relationship between husband and wife. Unfortunately, the RSV calls the sexual satisfaction husbands and wives owe one another 'conjugal rights' (v. 3) – which conjures up in the popular mind the idea that the husband (in particular) has a right to sex with his wife as and when he chooses. However, Paul's emphasis is rather on the *lack of rights* that husbands and wives each have over their own bodies. What we have here is not 'conjugal rights' but 'conjugal giving'. The husband should give himself to his wife because he has no 'right' to withhold his body, and likewise (note how men and women are treated equally throughout this chapter) the wife should give herself to her husband. In a Christian marriage, husband and wife are concerned not with what they can *get* but with what they must *give* to each other.

This 'conjugal giving' is essentially 'other-centred' and part of its purpose is to keep one's partner from 'immoralities'. It is not hard to follow Paul's reasoning here. If men or women who are used to sexual intimacy within marriage suddenly find themselves deprived of it – for example because one partner decides it is 'unspiritual' – they will be tempted to seek it elsewhere (and in Corinth were evidently giving in to the temptation). Whilst giving in to temptation is a sin, each husband nevertheless has to recognize that he is his wife's first line of defence against such sin, and the same is true for wives with regard to their husbands. In Corinth, some people

NOT TONIGHT DEAR...! I'VE GOT A THEOLOGICAL OBJECTION!

were apparently suggesting that all sexual activity was at best 'unspiritual'. Paul's response is to tell them that, on the contrary, for married people *giving up sexual activity* would be the unspiritual thing!

This conclusion is perhaps surprising, and down the centuries much so-called Christian teaching has suggested the exact opposite. Augustine's comments on this passage are illuminating:

> 'One could consider that it is not a sin for a married couple to have intercourse ... for the sake of the carnal pleasure involved ... had the apostle not added, "But I say this as a concession, not as a rule."' [6]

Augustine recognizes that Paul's message in vv.2-5 is that *sex is for pleasure* within marriage (and not just 'for children'). But Augustine had based his whole struggle towards conversion on the principle that sex was *always* sinful. So he seizes on v.6 with relief as an escape clause – Paul allows intercourse *only as a concession*! Unfortunately for the subsequent development of Christian thinking, Augustine misses the point entirely - the concession Paul allows is to *abstinence*, as is plain from v.5:

> 'Do not deprive one another (i.e. *withhold from sexual intercourse*), except perhaps by agreement for a time [...] And then come together again, that Satan might not tempt you through your lack of self-control.'

If Paul had meant what Augustine thought he meant, he would surely have written:

> 'Do not **come together**, except perhaps by agreement for a time [...] And then **withhold from one another again**, that Satan might not tempt you through your lack of self-control.'

Contrary to Augustine, Yves of Chartres and others, sex without marriage and marriage without sex are both, in biblical terms, sinful. Paul takes the obligation married people have to provide for one another sexually so seriously that the word we have translated 'deprive' in v.5 is the same word used in James 5:4 to describe defrauding workers from the wages due to them. Paul *does* allow a married couple to withhold from one another sexually if it is by mutual agreement for the express purpose of giving themselves to prayer. But this should only be for a short time, otherwise there is a danger that Satan will tempt one or the other to look for a sexual outlet outside the marriage. He does not allow an 'ascetic wedge' to be driven between physical pleasure and spiritual growth (cf. 1 Tim 4:4-5). Nor will he allow a false 'super-spirituality' to become an excuse to avoid the earthy aspects of human life.

As a *sensitive* pastor, Paul makes a limited concession to the Corinthian understanding of spirituality. However, as a *wise* pastor he emphasises it is 'not a command'. He does not advocate periods of 'sexual fasting' as a means to spiritual growth – on the contrary, needless abstinence leads not to self-control but Satanic temptation!

SUMMARY
Vv.1-6 are Paul's response to the suggestion by the 'ascetic' section of the congregation at Corinth that sex was best avoided. Whilst agreeing that some of the Corinthians would do well to avoid their present sexual activities, he disagrees that sexual abstinence is a route to true spirituality for all. Indeed for married couples the opposite is true - unwilling abstinence leads only to temptation. Husbands and wives should go on having sex because this is something they owe to one another and it will aid, rather than hinder, their spiritual growth.

THINKING IT THROUGH

1. Sex Matters
We now need to consider the implications of this for the married and the single. First, in marriage *sex matters a great deal*. Husband and wife have an obligation to provide for one another sexually and the path to true spirituality in marriage includes this provision. Of course, this has serious implications for our thinking about marriage. Long before we consider marrying someone – before we even have someone specific in mind to marry – we should think through the following points:

   1. I will be responsible for the lifelong sexual satisfaction of my spouse.

2. This is an obligation on a par with the other obligations of marriage.

3. To neglect this aspect of marriage is to deprive my spouse of something I owe them. It is equivalent to cheating or defrauding them.

4. To care for my spouse's sexual satisfaction will help keep them from temptation.

If you have not thought through these things, or if you do not feel you can live up to them, you are not ready for marriage yet. Paul's words in 1 Corinthians 7 show that you *must* consider these issues, if necessary by talking with an older Christian friend or pastor. It might be an idea if you jotted down now some of your reactions to what you have read so far and discussed them with other Christians. And, of course, you should also go back over the text of 1 Corinthians 7.

It may be, of course, that you already are married, in which case I hope that yours is a fruitful and happy relationship. However, it may also be that you recognize there are problems about sexuality in your marriage. May I suggest that you don't ignore these? You cannot use the excuse that yours is a Christian marriage so 'that sort of thing doesn't really matter.' The whole point of the opening verses of 1 Corinthians 7 is that these things matter very much in a Christian marriage because in that context they are part of our route to holiness.

Of course, sex is not the main thing in a marriage, nor is keeping one another from temptation the main thing in sex. We have to bear in mind that Paul is writing to a *particular* situation and therefore he does not say everything there is to say about sex and marriage. (For biblical 'light relief' you should read the *Song of Songs* and meditate on what that has to say.) However, sex has an importance which is often overlooked by Christians. It both expresses and creates the unity of marriage because by means of it 'the two become one flesh', and therefore it is also a warning light to tell of other problems in the relationship.

2. 'Other-centred' sexuality

Second, this passage presents us with the concept of 'other-centred' sexuality. Biblical thinking about sex starts not with what *I* like but with what the other likes. This comes out in Paul's statement about the ownership of our bodies (v.4). In marriage, as in the Christian life generally, we live for others and our proper aim in marriage is to please our spouse (vv.33- 34). (Of course, this has disadvantages in terms of Christian service which Paul is careful to highlight later in this chapter.) **It is most important to realize this, preferably *before* marriage take place, and to note that it applies in the area of sexuality as much as in every other area**.

This has some interesting implications, because in sex, as in many other matters, what pleases men and what pleases women are *complementary opposites*. What women like and what men like are related but different! In Genesis 2 (a chapter which has much to say about the nature and purpose of marriage) verse 18 states:

'Then the Lord God said, "It is not good that the man should be alone; I will make him a helper fit for him. "' (RSV)

The concept of the 'fit helper' is a fascinating one. It does not mean, as some seem to imagine, someone to do the man's washing-up. The term used for a 'helper' (Hebrew *ezer*, as in Ebenezer) frequently describes God in the Old Testament and the 'help' provided is of *strengthening* the person helped. But the phrase the RSV translates 'fit for' is literally 'as opposite to' the man. What the man needs to provide this 'help' is something *like* him but *different* from him. The animals are different, but not sufficiently like him. Eve is *like* him but she is significantly different from him. In Hebrew she is *ishshah* (woman), like

GOD SAID IT WAS THIS OR A DISHWASHER!

- but also not like – *ish* (man). She is a true help, but she is 'a helper as opposite to him'.

These opposites show in many ways, and are part of what makes relationships between men and women delightful and yet frustrating. In the area of sexuality they require particular awareness and care. Yet how many men and women know, much less *do*, what pleases the opposite sex *sexually*? Even when this happens, it is usually in a self-centred way as a means to what each can get out of it, rather than purely to please their partner.

It has to be said that this is particularly a problem for Christian women, especially the single. The female sexual response is more slowly aroused than the male's (though it may be correspondingly very powerful) and therefore women may be less generally aware of it in themselves. But Christian women often feel an additional pressure not to express their sexuality. Combined with our cultural trend to 'unisexuality', the result is a tendency to act and dress in ways which minimize women's sexual identity, *not* in obedience to the injunctions to modesty in 1 Timothy 2:9 or 1 Peter 3:3-4 but because they are more 'comfortable' that way. This is not a problem if they do not want a relationship with someone of the *opposite* sex. But if, as is generally the case, they want to marry, then they must recognize that marriage is essentially a *sexual* relationship which takes into account what the *other* likes. Of course, if they have a 'self-centred' rather than 'other-centred' approach to sexuality, women may condemn men as having 'sex on the brain' – and indeed *from a Christian woman's perspective* they do. But this is like English people condemning all Americans as 'loud' – they are only loud if we judge them by English standards. Men are *not* women – they are 'opposite to' women, and Christian women need to understand that this applies to sex in particular. An 'other-centred' sexuality doesn't necessarily mean women dressing in leather mini-skirts – perhaps just a little less 'Doctor Marten's' and a little more 'Dorothy Perkins'. Sometimes a change of wardrobe goes a long way in moving from a 'self-centred' to an 'other-centred' sexuality.

Of course, similar problems affect Christian men, who are also 'self-centred' in their sexuality. They wonder why women aren't more aware of what men find attractive, when very few men have any idea what *women* find attractive – much less try to live up to it. It also has to be said that one of the reasons why Christian women have difficulties with male sexuality is that men often make lousy lovers. Female sexuality depends on the opposites of male sexuality for its arousal. Men need little more than the opportunity, the confidence and a basic attraction to the woman concerned. A woman needs communication and atmosphere. She needs an awareness that her *whole* life contributes to her sexual feelings, which is why *commitment* is so important to her. Above all, she needs the three 'Ts': Time, Touch and Tenderness. For a man, sexual activity is a *relief* from the routine of daily life. For a woman it grows (or fails to grow) *out of* the routine of daily life. It is this *context*, and the failure of men to attend to it, that women often refer to when they complain about the lack of 'romance' in their lives.

Within marriage, lack of awareness combines with lack of communication to make the marriage bed a sexual battleground. So many marriages seem to consist of a mutual and yet unspoken frustration: 'If only she wouldn't ...', 'If only he would ...'. And often these frustrations result from issues which were never considered by one partner or the other before marriage. Communication means talking to one another, not someone else, and husbands and wives need to be able to tell one another what they like and dislike sexually if they are to avoid mutual frustration. But good communication between the sexes needs to begin long before marriage is contemplated and it is enhanced by being 'other-centred'. Those who wish to have a relationship with a member of the opposite sex should spend some time considering what those 'opposites' involve. 'Other-centred' sexuality requires awareness, commitment and self-giving, but in the end it can be one of the many ways in which, by losing our own life we end up by gaining it.

Chapter 3

Is there a Gift of Singleness?

1 Corinthians 7:7

⁷For I wish all men to be as I myself am. But each has his own gift of grace from God, one this, another that.

This verse concludes Paul's advice to married couples and leads into his remarks on other issues in the rest of the chapter. It is commonly assumed that the first part of this verse means he would prefer everyone to be single. The second part is then assumed to indicate that some (those very few people, like Paul, who enjoy it) have the 'gift of singleness' whilst others (almost everyone else, especially those who don't enjoy being single) don't.[7]

On further thought, however, both these assumptions are unlikely. To begin with, the verse as a whole would set Paul against his God, who apparently didn't give enough people the gift of singleness. Also, if Paul wants people to remain single, his advice in vv.9 and 36 is very odd. One commentator highlights the apparent contradiction as follows:

> 'V.7a reads, "I wish all men to be as I am." The words are obviously Paul's ... however, in this context they do not reflect Paul's position. Paul does not wish all men to be unmarried.'[8]

There is, however, another explanation available to us. V.7 is grammatically linked to v.6 by the word translated 'For' (Greek *de*). Paul's comment in v.6 is that he will allow short periods of sexual abstinence as a *concession* to Corinthian spirituality. But when he says in v.7 '*For* I wish all men to be as I myself am', he means 'as I am in Christ', namely free from the spiritual rigorism that denies physical pleasures. He does not command abstinence 'For' he serves Christ in liberty. Though the underlying Greek is different, we may compare this with his speech to Agrippa in Acts: 'I would to God that ... all who hear me this day might become *such as I am* – except for these chains." (26:29, RSV)

We should then understand the second half of this verse to emphasize that this liberty is experienced in various ways, depending on the 'gift of grace' (literally *charisma*) that God bestows. Verse 8 continues this theme further with Paul's advice to widows and others: some of them may choose to remain single, others should marry, depending not on 'rules' but on their circumstances and God's 'gift' to them.

But still some may ask, 'How do I know which "gift" God has given me? ' More particularly, if you are single and not enjoying it does this mean you don't have the 'gift of singleness'? It is tempting to answer 'Yes' and to suggest that this means either God has a marriage partner lined up for you or that your life is on 'hold' until you find someone. But if this is true for the single, what does it mean if you are *married* and not enjoying it? Does this mean you don't have the 'gift of marriage'? If it does then you are in even more serious trouble than the unhappily single. Not only are you unhappily married, you shouldn't be married at all (or, as is tempting to think, you shouldn't be married to *this* person)! In reply, we have to say emphatically that *enjoying your condition in life cannot be a safe guide as to whether it is God's will for you*. If you find this hard to believe, think of Christ's words in Gethsemane: 'Father ... remove this cup from me; nevertheless not my will, but thine, be done.' (Luke 22:42,RSV)

What does Paul mean here by a 'gift of grace'? In the context, he certainly *does* seem to include our *different inclinations*, some inclining towards marriage, others not. But these inclinations are worked out in circumstances which are sometimes beyond our control, and these *circumstances* are also part of God's 'gift' to us. Paul's immediate emphasis, however, is not so much on the nature of the gift as on the *differences* between us and the freedom we have in Christ to act on these differences – 'one this, another that'. He is not so concerned about the way we *experience* the differences, some enjoying life, others perhaps not enjoying it so much, as with the fact that Christian spirituality may be expressed by more than one lifestyle. The meaning of v.7 seems to be that

Paul wants everyone to be like him in *principle* (i.e. free in Christ) but acknowledges that this means they will differ from him in *practice* (some marrying, others remaining single). Understanding the verse in this way makes it intelligible both on its own and in its context.

There is not a 'gift of singleness' in the sense of a psychological constitution which means enjoying being celibate and living on your own, any more than there is a 'gift of marriage' which means having a wonderful sex-life and always enjoying the company of your spouse and children. Of course, some people are like this, but enormous numbers (perhaps most) simply aren't. The 'gift' we have from God referred to in 1 Corinthians 7 is our life situation – our total selves and the context in which we are placed. The response called for is to trust and serve him in that context and so become more like Christ.

Chapter 4

Marriage and Death

1 Corinthians 7:8-9

[8]So I say to the unmarried and the widows, it is good for them if they remain as I do. [9]But if they are not exercising self-control, let them marry; for it is better to marry than to burn.

In spite of what we have said in the previous chapter, there is a general opinion in evangelical circles that here Paul lays it on the line for single people: if you don t like being single, get married! Commenting on these verses, Phillip Jensen and Tony Payne write:

> 'One of the primary motivations for marriage (in fact, the only one given in this passage) is sex. If we find we cannot control our sexual desires, we should marry for "it is better to marry than to burn with passion ".'[9]

In a similar vein, Peter Bolt writes:

> '...if a person is unmarried and finding it difficult the choice is there to marry.'[10]

I would count all three writers as friends of mine and they are excellent Bible teachers, but here I think they come too close to saying there is no reason why any Christian should remain single who doesn't want to. The difficulty, of course, is that *marriageability* involves more than *availability*. To use a different example, there is no reason why anyone should ever be unemployed. There are jobs available, if only the unemployed would take them, and Christians are commanded to be 'ready for any honest work' (Titus 3:1). Unfortunately, like another

Christian friend of mine, you could find that the only job you are offered is in a warehouse packing pornographic magazines. (Actually, he took it, though I'm not sure it was what Paul meant!) But if you have any discernment, any ambitions, any special skills or training you would like to use, or even a minimum wage you want to earn, finding a job may be a little more difficult. So for the single Christian, there are other single Christians out there wanting to marry - maybe even wanting to marry you – but this doesn't necessarily mean you are wrong to have other ideas.

A lot of people believe Paul was particularly advising single people to get married if they found sexual temptation a problem. Thus Jensen and Payne go on to say, '... those who do not have the gift of being able to control their sexual appetites *should* marry with a clear conscience'.[11] But many frustrated single Christians will tell you they just can't find the right person. Even Jensen and Payne admit that 'finding a partner in our society is not always easy'.[12] Are these people disobeying God, being foolish or, as Jensen and Payne suggest, just being fussy? As a single person myself, I used to be troubled by the fact that the Bible appeared to be telling me to do something which in practice I found impossible. However, a closer look at the passage suggests that Paul is not saying what it is usually assumed he was saying and he is not addressing the people it is usually assumed he was addressing.

WHAT IS HE SAYING?

In v.7 Paul said that he wanted everyone 'to be' (Greek, *einai*) 'as I myself am' (Gr, *hōs kai hemauton*). He begins these next verses by telling the unmarried and widows, 'it is good for them if *they remain*' (Gr, *meinōsin*) 'as I do' (Gr, *hōs kagō*). The difference is small, but I would argue it is significant. In the first case he is saying 'It is good for *all* to be as I am in Christ, i.e. free.' In the second he is saying 'It is good for *some* to remain as I am in practice, i.e. single.' We should not confuse the two and assume Paul is saying it is good for all to be single.

Nevertheless, when it comes to applying vv.8-9, it is often overlooked that here *Paul recommends singleness, not marriage.* It is a little odd, to say the least, that some people turn Paul's recommendation to remain single into an instruction to get married! Our first conclusion from these verses should surely be that *no one has to marry* – even if they are sexually frustrated. We all have the freedom to remain single and, for reasons we will see later, Paul believes it is sometimes good if we do.

But still people will reply, 'Paul is only recommending that you remain single if you are not struggling with temptation. "If you burn with passion," he says you should marry.' This interpretation is attractive to the person who hopes their frustrations indicate it is God's plan that they *will* marry, but it owes more to *Mills and Boon* than to the Apostle Paul. His meaning in v.9 is often assumed to be as follows:

'... **if they are finding sexual self-control difficult**, they should marry; for it is better to marry than **to burn with passion**.'

But though Paul talks about 'burning' he says nothing specifically about 'passion'. What he actually says to the unmarried and widows is:

'...**if they ARE NOT EXERCISING self-control**, let them marry; for it is better to marry than **to burn**.'

Paul is not writing to people who are *struggling* to control themselves but to people who are *failing* to control themselves – and there is all the difference in the world between the two. A little later in the same letter, Paul compares his own self-control with that of an athlete:

'Every athlete exercises self-control in all things. They do it to receive a perishable wreath, but we an imperishable. Well, I do not run aimlessly, I do not box as one beating the air; but I pommel my body and subdue it, lest after preaching to others I myself should be disqualified.' (9:25-27, RSV)

The word for an athlete here is literally 'one who agonizes', and the agony of an athlete includes the battle for self-control. Look at the faces during a race – athletes may well be tempted to give up, but if they want to succeed they don't. Instead, as Paul says, they exercise self-control – they keep going for the sake of the prize at the end!

Exactly the same applies to single Christians who struggle with sexual temptation. Do they want to give up? Of course they do!

But does the fact that they struggle - even agonize - mean they *should* give up? Of course not! Instead, they should go on *exercising self-control*. The answer to sexual temptation *must* be self-control, not marriage, otherwise what would married people do who are sexually tempted?

So Paul isn't telling frustrated single people to marry. (If anything, he is saying it is good if they remain single.) But he *is* telling *someone* to marry, so who is it?

WHOM IS HE ADDRESSING?

At the beginning of v.8 Paul refers to 'the unmarried and the widows.' It is generally assumed that this means 'those-who-have-never-married and widows'. However, there is some evidence to suggest that the word 'unmarried' actually means 'widowers' when paired with 'widows' (Fee, pp.287- 288). In v.11 the same word is used to describe a married woman separated from her husband, so it certainly doesn't *have* to mean 'never married'. Moreover, if we assume that Paul means 'widowers and widows' it neatly separates the advice here for those whose marriages have been ended by death from the advice to those who have never yet married ('the virgins') beginning at v.25. Of course, 'neatness' does not prove our suggestion but it lends weight to it.

But whoever Paul is addressing, they are described as 'not exercising self-control'. In the context, this can only mean they are involved in wrongful sexual activity. The surprise is that Paul doesn't tell them to stop it - he tells them to *marry*! And this helps us understand who these people are that Paul is addressing. He would not suggest that a Christian should marry anyone unsuitable. In particular, the marriage partner must be another Christian. (In v.39 he says that a widow is 'free to be married to whom she wishes, *only in the Lord.*') Yet these people could legitimately marry when in fact they are behaving immorally. It makes sense to suggest that they are Christians - widowers and widows - who have found potential marriage partners and are involved in sexual relationships with them, but have held back from marrying.

Yet why would anyone who *could* marry remain unmarried? The answer probably lies in the expectations of others. In a church where some members were keen on other-worldly asceticism, widowers and widows might have felt under considerable pressure not to remarry. Even today, some people feel the bereaved should wait a 'decent ' interval before remarrying. (And indeed it *is* wise not to marry 'on the rebound', whether it is from a bereavement or a broken relationship.) But it is always better to marry than to sin – and Paul is concerned not with the 'decent interval' but with holy living. When he adds 'it is better to marry than to burn' this doesn't mean 'burning with unfulfilled desire'. Those who are 'not exercising self-control' are *fulfilling* their desires! But Paul uses the same expression in 2 Corinthians 11:29 where he asks, 'Who is weak and I am not weak? Who is made to stumble and I do not *burn?*' There is no thought here of romantic passion. Paul is talking about the *shame* which results from sin - even his own shame at the sin of his converts. The Christians at Corinth who, instead of exercising self-control, are having sex outside marriage suffer the 'burning shame' *now* of knowing they are doing something wrong and they may suffer the 'purifying fire' of judgement in the *future* (cf. 3:15). But Paul does not condemn them, he liberates them! Rather than going on sinning, these Christians should simply marry. Then they could enjoy their relationships to the full.

GOD AND THE BEREAVED

Clearly there is a lot more that could be said about widows and bereavement and indeed the Bible has much to say about God's special concern for widows and orphans. James sums it up thus:

'Religion that is pure and undefiled before God and the Father is this: to visit orphans and widows in their affliction, and to keep oneself unstained from the world.' (1:27, RSV)

Paul is concerned with one particular aspect of life after bereavement, namely whether it is possible or appropriate to marry again. His answer is a resounding 'Yes', but the timing of this should not depend on social or religious convention. The important thing, as we will see in the case of the 'never-married' later, is the holiness of the couple concerned.

Beyond that, there are no hard and fast rules. People who have been bereaved of a marriage partner can choose to marry or not, depending on their inclination and circumstances. The lesson from this passage is that they should not be needlessly deterred from marriage either by other people's expectations or their own loyalty to a former spouse. In his argument with the Sadducees about the resurrection, Jesus showed that marriage is not *eternally* binding (Luke 20:27-40).[13] If a widower or widow finds a potential marriage partner, the *right* choice is to practise holiness and avoid sin.

Chapter 5

Marriage, Divorce and Separation

1 Corinthians 7:10-11

[10]And for the married I command (not I but the Lord) that a woman should not separate from her husband [11]– but if she separates, let her remain unmarried or be reconciled to her husband – and a man should not put away his wife.

WHEN THE GRASS IS NOT GREENER

There is a tendency amongst the unmarried to assume that the grass is greener on the married side of the fence, and indeed it should be since God has made us for marriage. But the world is a fallen and sinful place and Christians share the effects of this in the same way as others. As a result, there are not only unhappily single people but unhappily married people. Without a knowledge of the Bible we might assume that the *Christian* answer to such unhappiness would be divorce. This, after all, would seem to be the compassionate and loving response to people who find themselves tied in an unhappy relationship – anything else smacks of legalism.

It is therefore a shock to find that at this point Jesus was uncompromising in upholding the 'sanctity' of marriage. This is surely why Paul adds to his command in v.10 the comment 'not I but the Lord'. There would otherwise be many in Paul's day tempted to write off this prohibition as a personal opinion of the Apostle, just as there are many today who still cannot accept Jesus really meant what he said.

JESUS AND DIVORCE

However, it is not Jesus' attitude to divorce which is radical so much as his view of marriage, which goes right back to the creation of the human race. In Matthew 19:3-9 we read:

> 'And Pharisees came up to him and tested him by asking, "Is it lawful to divorce one's wife for any cause?" He answered, "Have you not read that he who made them from the beginning made them male and female, and said, 'For this reason a man shall leave his father and mother and be joined to his wife, and the two shall become one flesh'? So they are no longer two but one flesh. What therefore God has joined together, let not man put asunder." They said to him, "Why then did Moses command one to give a certificate of divorce, and to put her away?" He said to them, "For your hardness of heart Moses allowed you to divorce your wives, but from the beginning it was not so. And I say to you: whoever divorces his wife, except for unchastity, and marries another, commits adultery."' (RSV)

In referring back to Genesis 2:24 for his understanding of marriage Jesus brings out two important points. First, **Genesis 2 is as much about the creation of marriage as it is about the creation of the human race**. This is vital for our understanding of the relationships between male and female. The relationship between Adam and Eve was *first and foremost* one of *husband and wife*. We must not generalize from *this* relationship to male-female relationships *outside* marriage. Second, **Genesis 2 establishes the permanence of marriage**. Adam and Eve were joined together not by a whim of their own but by the action of God. Jesus reminds us we should not interfere with an institution God has created. From the very beginning marriage has a 'high status' which should govern our thinking.

DIVORCE AND THE OLD TESTAMENT

As Jesus also points out, divorce is not part of God's plan for marriage but an accommodation to human sin so as to limit the damage it does. It is surprising when we look at the Pentateuch (Genesis-Deuteronomy) how little the Old Testament Law has to say on the matter. In fact the 'law' to which the Pharisees refer consists of just four verses in Deuteronomy 24:1-4 which not so much 'command' divorce as limit remarriage. (They actually forbid a man remarrying the wife he divorced who has since remarried and been divorced by her second husband - if you can follow that!)

The overall verdict of the Old Testament on divorce is entirely negative. In Malachi 2:13-16 there is a scathing condemnation of Israel's easy-going attitude in this respect:

> 'You cover the LORD's altar with tears, with weeping and groaning because he no longer regards the offering or accepts it with favour at your hand. You ask, Why does he not? Because the LORD was witness to the covenant between you and the wife of your youth, to whom you have been faithless, though she is your companion and your wife by covenant. Has not the one God made and sustained for us the spirit of life? And what does he desire? Godly offspring. So take heed to yourselves, and let none be faithless to the wife of his youth. "For I hate divorce, says the LORD the God of Israel, and covering one's garment with violence, says the LORD of hosts. So take heed to yourselves and do not be faithless."' (RSV)

MARRIAGE AND COVENANT
The passage from Malachi above shows that marriage is regarded as a *covenant* between a man and a woman. That is to say, it is a

relationship of *personal obligation*. This helps explain why divorce was so hated by God, since the term 'covenant' also describes the relationship between God and his people. Moreover, the covenant between God and Israel in the Old Testament is itself pictured as a marriage. Jeremiah (31:32) describes Israel as God's husband by covenant. Hosea makes great play on the nature of God as the faithful husband and Israel as the faithless wife. And Ezekiel 16 contains extraordinary, even erotic, imagery to describe this relationship:

> 'And you grew up and became tall and arrived at full maidenhood; your breasts were formed, and your hair had grown; yet you were naked and bare. When I passed by you again and looked upon you, behold, you were at the age for love; and I spread my skirt over you, and covered your nakedness: yea, I plighted my troth to you and **entered into a covenant with you**, says the Lord GOD and you became mine.'
> (16:7-8, RSV)

This picture is carried over into the New Testament ('Testament' just being an old-fashioned word for 'Covenant') where Jesus is described by John the Baptist as the 'Bridegroom' (John 3:29). Jesus also called himself the 'Bridegroom':

> 'And Jesus said to them, "Can the wedding guests fast while the bridegroom is with them? As long as they have the bridegroom with them, they cannot fast."' (Mark 2:19, RSV)

Bearing in mind the Old Testament background, this is an extraordinary statement. Jesus claims to be what God is – the husband of Israel! In Ephesians 5:22-33 this is made even more explicit. Paul says that the human covenant of marriage pictures the relationship between Christ and his redeemed people, the Church. In vv.31-32 Paul quotes Genesis 2:24, drawing together the threads of the Biblical picture:

> '"For this reason a man shall leave his father and mother and be joined to his wife, and the two shall become one flesh." This mystery is a profound one, and I am saying that it refers to Christ and the church...' (RSV)

At the end of the Bible, the true marriage is not that between a man and a woman but between Christ and the Church:

> 'And I saw the holy city, new Jerusalem, coming down out of heaven from God, prepared as a bride adorned for her husband …'
> (Revelation 21:2, RSV)

COVENANT AND SALVATION

This close connection between the 'covenant of marriage' and the 'covenant of salvation', is the reason why *divorce is such an impossibility*. Put bluntly, if we can divorce one another, God can divorce us. Our salvation could never be assured because we are a faithless bride like Israel. But the faithfulness of God to unfaithful Israel is a central message of the Old Testament. The first part of Isaiah 50:1 asks:

> 'Where is your mother's bill of divorce, with which I put her away? Or which of my creditors is it to whom I have sold you?' (50:1a, RSV)

The second part of the verse answers that Israel has been put away (i.e. sent into the Exile) for *her* sins, not because of a change of mind on God's part:

> 'Behold, for your iniquities you were sold, and for your transgressions your mother was put away.' (50:1b, RSV)

But this cannot be a permanent state of affairs. God redeems his people, and so we read in Isaiah 62:4:

> 'You shall no more be termed Forsaken, and your land shall no more be termed Desolate; but you shall be called My delight is in her, and your land Married; for the LORD delights in you, and your land shall be married.' (RSV)

To accept divorce as a normal part of marriage would be to contradict the biblical picture of salvation. Marriage is instituted by God, not invented by man, and if we want the relationship between Christ and the Church to be pictured *by* marriage then divorce cannot be part of it. Only adultery or (as we will see later) desertion with its implication of adultery, can be allowed to break the marriage bond. And, of course, amongst Christians deliberate adultery is unthinkable as an excuse for remarrying.

Paul's command to the unhappily married that they may not divorce is unequivocal, but it is not based on legalism, either on his part or on the part of Jesus. It is based on the entire flow of Biblical thinking, not only about marriage but about salvation.

IMPLICATIONS
Where, then, does this leave unhappy Christian couples like those in 1 Corinthians 7? Unhappy marriages remain a serious human problem, and it is not enough simply to review what the Bible teaches. We have to apply it compassionately.

First, Paul tells us that if both husband and wife wish to act Christianly then divorce is not an option. But, second, we learn that in extreme cases separation *is* possible, even though remarriage is not. Women, in particular, do not have to stay in a situation where they are in physical danger. If things are so bad that a couple can no longer live together under the same roof then separation would be the lesser evil. We would be justified in suggesting there is serious need for growth in their Christianity if such were the case, but separation is not a disciplinary offence in the Church. Paul does not threaten separated couples with excommunication – he simply reminds them they remain married and cannot marry anyone else. This leads to the third point, that in unhappy Christian marriages, reconciliation, not remarriage, is the goal for which we should aim.

For local churches there are important lessons also. In any reasonably large church at a given time there are bound to be couples whose marriages are going through difficulty. The congregation has a responsibility to be sensitive and yet, if necessary, firm. Marriage, like any relationship between two sinful people, will never be without problems and an open and honest attitude in the church will help couples negotiate these. If the worst happens and a couple separate, the church must realize that this is an option for Christians, albeit an undesirable and painful one. What the church must not do is allow compassion to spill over into license and begin to see divorce as a Christian option. It is not – we have Jesus' word for it.

Naturally, all this should make us think very carefully about marriage! In this respect, surely the only thing worse than being unhappily single is being unhappily married. We should 'look before we leap' and we should remember that where marriage is concerned there is no reserve parachute! If this chapter has made you think, I am sure Paul has succeeded in his aim.

Chapter 6

Mixed Marriages and Desertion

1 Corinthians 7:12-16

[12]To the rest I say (not the Lord), if any brother has a wife who is an unbeliever, and she is pleased to live with him, let him not send her away. [13]And if any woman has a husband who is an unbeliever, and this man is pleased to live with her, let her not send the man away. [14]For the unbelieving husband is sanctified by the woman, and the unbelieving wife is sanctified by the brother – otherwise your children are unclean, but now they are sanctified. [15]But if the unbeliever separates, let him go. The brother or the sister is not bound in such a case, but God called you to peace. [16]How do you know, O woman, if you will save the man? Or how do you know, O man, if you will save the woman?

WHAT IS THE PROBLEM?

It is a fact of life that not all 'Christian' marriages are between two Christians. Very often one partner (usually the wife) is converted and the other is not. What is Paul's advice to those in 'mixed marriages'? The concern in Corinth is clearly not exactly shared by us today. Today the question is, 'How can I persuade my partner to believe?' For the people in Corinth the question was rather more stark: 'Should I get a divorce?' We may be relieved to hear that, though he cannot quote Jesus on the matter, Paul's answer is 'No'. Nevertheless, it is worth asking why the question arose.

It seems from v.14 that some people in Corinth may have suggested Christians in mixed marriages were in danger of being 'corrupted' by their unbelieving partners. This is not as unlikely a suggestion as it may sound. In the books of Ezra and Nehemiah we read that for the Exiles returning from Babylon in 534 BC, mixed marriages were a burning issue and many of them 'put away' their pagan spouses. (The problem was not so much that the wives were 'foreign' as that they were unbelievers, cf. Deuteronomy 7:4 etc.) It may be that some people in Corinth were aware of this precedent and now felt that Christians should do the same.

The Corinthians, however, are first-generation Christians. Whilst it would be wrong for them deliberately to marry unbelievers (see 7:39), they cannot act like sixth century BC Jews. It is not surprising, then, that Paul takes a different line. The first issue, he says, is whether the unbeliever wishes to stay. If he or she does, then the covenant of marriage takes priority over the problem of unbelief. Secondly, the belief of the Christian spouse is more significant than unbelief of the partner. Far from the believer being 'corrupted', the unbeliever is 'sanctified' (i.e. 'made holy') through the believer. Paul offers as a precedent the position of children. It seems he is referring here not just to the children of the mixed marriages but to the children of all the church families in Corinth and he takes it for granted that everyone agrees they are 'holy'. This is not quite the same as being 'saved' – it is still an open question in v.16 whether the unbelieving husband or wife will be saved or not, and presumably the same applied to the children who were too young to express belief independently of their parents. But it *does* mean they are neither 'unclean' (v.14) nor merely 'spiritually neutral'.

This may cause discomfort for Baptists who like to deal in strict black and whites when it comes to mature belief. On the other hand, it isn't quite enough to allow Anglicans to be overconfident about infant baptism. The trouble is, we simply don't know exactly what Paul meant here, nor what he felt was the 'cash value' of this 'sanctification'. Perhaps he had in mind something like what Jesus refers to in Matthew 23:17 where he speaks of 'the Temple that sanctifies the gold'. Clearly it was felt that a 'holiness' *independent of belief* passed from the greater (the Temple) to the lesser (the gold). In a similar way, perhaps, the believing spouse has this effect on the family, even if the rest are unbelievers. The key point is they are not 'unclean' nor will they corrupt the believer. Indeed, there is a good chance that through the presence of the believer they will themselves come to belief. (1 Peter 3:1-4 has some good, if surprising, advice on how to convert an unbelieving spouse.)

WHAT ABOUT DESERTION?

There is, however, the unpleasant possibility that the unbelieving spouse will not recognize the Christian principles by which the believer lives. He or she may even leave the marriage because of them. What is a believer to do if deserted by an unbelieving spouse?

Here again Paul has no direct word from Jesus, but his advice is to let the unbeliever go. There is no obligation on the Christian partner to hold on to a marriage which is being broken up by the actions of someone who is not open to Christian persuasion or discipline. In this case, Paul says, 'the brother or the sister is not bound'. Here I *disagree* with Fee (pp. 302 – 303) who says Paul would not allow remarriage after such a desertion. We should bear in mind that desertion would almost certainly be followed by adultery on the part of the unbeliever and Jesus himself allowed divorce on such grounds. Moreover, if we compare the advice to partners of believers in v.11 with the advice to partners of unbelievers in v.15 there is an evident contrast:

V.11 '...but if she separates, **let her remain unmarried**...	V.15 'But if the unbeliever separates, **let him go**.
...**or be reconciled** to her husband'	**The brother or the sister is not bound** in such a case.'

With believers Paul is careful to emphasise that separation does not allow remarriage – it is a temporary situation with the hope of reunion. With unbelievers, however, separation is to be accepted and leaves the deserted believer free – the deserted Christian is not 'bound' (literally 'in bondage' or 'in slavery') to their ex-partner. Of course, we should not *seek* desertion – the covenant of marriage is still a covenant, even with an unbelieving partner. But we cannot persuade or coerce someone beyond a certain point. Indeed, in case some conscientious Christians felt that the possibility of saving their spouse was a reason for holding on to the marriage at all costs, Paul seems to emphasize that sometimes a marriage must be allowed to end. Believers cannot know whether they will save the unbelieving husband or wife. In the end, God has called us to live in peace, and that may include the peace of letting an unwilling or unfaithful partner go.[14]

IMPLICATIONS

These verses are particularly helpful in knowing how to respond if
someone was divorced or remarried before becoming a Christian,
or if someone becomes a Christian whilst in a long-standing
relationship with a non-christian. It is not possible to undo the
past, nor as Paul shows, is it always advisable to change the
present. Conversion allows us to draw a line across a person's life
and say 'From here they start again.' For people who have
divorced and remarried after conversion, their *present* marriage is
the one that counts.

Similarly, the person who is not married but is living with a
non-christian partner need not necessarily break off the
relationship. Frequently, they are in what the Australians call a
'de facto' marriage. (It would be a mistake to call it 'living in sin',
as if the absence of a marriage ceremony were the only problem in
their lives. Even married people can 'live in sin'!) On the other
hand, the Christian partner would be wise to raise the question of
marriage at some stage since he or she would want to introduce
the element of 'covenant' on his or her side of the relationship.
Also it must be remembered that non-christians often choose
'open' relationships precisely because they want to be free to leave
at some stage. It would be better, if a break must come, for it to
happen sooner rather than later, and raising the question of
marriage may be one way to resolve the issue. Generally in an
open relationship if the new convert behaves 'Christianly' their
partner will either walk away or move closer to belief.

For people who divorced before conversion but have *not*
remarried, the situation is slightly more complex. Are they
effectively single and free to remarry, or are they merely separated
and bound to remain as they are? Each person must think this
through carefully. However, my own conclusion is that, unless
there is real possibility of reconciliation with the former spouse,
the implication of Scripture is that they are to be counted as single
and may remarry. Scripture contains many examples, from
Rahab the harlot (who, it appears, married the great-grandfather
of David – Matt 1:4) to Paul himself, of people who were able to
put a sinful past behind them. Nevertheless, I would advise that
such remarriage waited until they had grown substantially in
their Christian life. Having made a mistake once, it would be
better for them to learn about being Christian before they took on

the responsibilities of choosing and living with a new spouse.

What this passage shows is that divorce, and subsequent remarriage, *are* possible where either or both partners in a marriage have acted unchristianly in breaking the marriage covenant through adultery or desertion. If the person concerned is someone who became a Christian after committing such an action it calls for repentance and an acknowledgement of the wonderful grace of God in wiping out past sins. Even if they committed such actions *as a Christian*, the grace and forgiveness of God is still available to them. They may even be accepted back by their partner. Adultery *allows* divorce but it does not *demand* it, as is shown by the example of God in relation to Israel. However, someone who has simply been betrayed or deserted by a partner should be treated with compassion on the part of the church, rather than be bound by a covenant they are unable to enforce.

The good news is that Christ is greater than our marital conundrums. He sanctifies the partners and children in our relationships, even when they do not share our belief. We may or may not be the cause of their salvation - that is ultimately for God to decide. But we are not called to endless anxiety and striving in this respect. Rather 'God has called you to peace'.

Chapter 7

Be what you Are

1 Corinthians 7:17-24

[17]Only as the Lord assigned to each, as God called each, so continue to walk – and so I command in all the churches. [18]Was anyone circumcised when called? Let him not remove the mark of circumcision. Or was anyone uncircumcised when called? Let him not be circumcised. [19]Circumcision is nothing, and uncircumcision is nothing, but keeping the commandments of God. [20]Let each remain as called, when called. [21]Were you called as a slave? Don't let it trouble you, though if indeed you are able to become free, rather make use of it. [22]For the one called as a slave in the Lord is free in the Lord. So also the one called as free is a slave of Christ. [23]You were bought with a price. Do not become slaves of men! [24]As each was called, brethren, in this state abide with God.

GOD'S CALLING

So far, Paul has been talking about sex and marriage, singleness and divorce. Why does he suddenly start talking about circumcision and slavery? The answer is that when you are trying to make a point about one subject it is sometimes easier to talk about something else, especially if the people you are talking to have rather fixed ideas on the topic in question.

Circumcision was a big issue in many of Paul's churches, but Corinth seems to have been an exception – the subject is only mentioned here. Paul is thus able to make a point about marriage by referring to something on which his hearers agreed with him: 'Circumcision is nothing, and uncircumcision is nothing, but keeping the commandments of God.' The big issue at Corinth concerning sex and marriage was *to what extent people should change their present behaviour* – should the married cut down on sex, should the widowed marry, should the unhappy separate, should the non-christian be divorced? Paul's first response to all these questions is 'Stay as you are!' because, as with circumcision, what matters is not your outward condition but your service of God.

Circumcision and slavery represented two of the great divides in the world of Paul's day – religious and social. The circumcised could, on the one hand, proudly claim to be the people of the true God. On the other hand, they were subject to a certain amount of social ostracism and ridicule. When answering nature's call or joining in the 'keep fit' classes at the gymnasium it was hard to disguise the fact that they lacked what most other men had got. So some people apparently went to great lengths (if we can use that expression) to stretch the circumcised foreskin. Slavery was a similar issue. Slaves were not necessarily mistreated, nor were they beaten three times a day. A slave could have great responsibility in the household and even have authority over the master's children. But at the end of the day, slaves were slaves and the free were free.

There must have been many Christians in Corinth who were tempted to think that if they could just change their circumstances they would have a better relationship with God. The circumcised may have worried that they bore the sign of the *Old* covenant. Surely God would bless them more if they didn't? On the other hand, the uncircumcised may have had the sneaking suspicion that they hadn't gone far enough with God. If only they would take the step of circumcision they would be closer to him. The slaves must have wondered about the opportunities for service they would have if only they were free, whilst those who were free may have wondered if they should bring themselves under human authority in their spiritual lives. Paul's advice to them and us is the same: 'Forget it!'

That the quality of our relationship with God is not determined by morally neutral circumstances can be shown by one simple fact: *God calls people to himself in those circumstances.*[15] If it were impossible to be a slave and serve God, he would have made sure the slave was free before calling him – but he didn't. In any case, as Paul points out, slavery and freedom are relative concepts. The Christian slave has a freedom the free non-christian does not enjoy. The free Christian has a Master who is more to be obeyed than even the owner of the slave. Similarly, under the New Covenant, the length of one's foreskin counts for nothing as regards our closeness to God or our ability to serve him. What matters is what we do with our lives, not how we look below the waist. God knew what we were like when he called us to become Christians and we don't have to change *anything* which is not actually sinful. Rather, Paul says, in the state in which we were called, we can 'abide' with God. He was not put off by our situation – why should we be?

LIVING LIFE NOW

What this means for marriage is obvious – we don't have to change anything! The married can stay married, the single can stay single and both can serve God as they are. Rather than worrying about *changing* our lives, we should concentrate on *living* them. Suppose, for example, you are unhappily single. Are you any different from someone who was unhappily a slave? The answer is 'No', but God knew what he was doing when he called the slave to himself as a slave, and he knew what he was doing when he called you to himself as single. This doesn't mean you have to pretend to enjoy being single, any more than the slave had to pretend to enjoy being a slave. It *does* mean you should concentrate on life now. Quite possibly you will marry at some time in the future, but equally possibly you may not. It may be that your struggles with singleness are part of the way God is moulding you to make you more like Christ (see Romans 8:28-29). And remember, there are unhappily married people who also face their daily struggles.

Of course, just because God called us as single – or married, or a slave – doesn't mean change is impossible. The slave is told that if the opportunity for freedom comes along he can use it.[16] If a potential marriage partner appears I don't have to refuse the opportunity on the grounds that I was single when I became a Christian. But it is important not to waste my whole life simply because no marriage partner has appeared *yet*. Today is, indeed, the first day of the rest of my life. It may also be the last, so I should abide in it with God and serve him to the best of my ability, confident that he has charge of my life and knows what he is doing even in the situations I find most difficult.

GOD THE SOVEREIGN
The underlying principle in Paul's argument is the awesome Sovereignty of God. Ultimately it is he who determines our situation and he who calls us to himself. This allows us confidence even in our difficulties – God *knows*, and he knows what he is doing. By moving the subject away from sex and marriage Paul challenges us to lift our eyes from our problems and consider the principles involved: am I thinking *Christianly?* Beyond my immediate concern lies the 'upward call' of God to eternal life (Phil 3:14). Whether the process by which God brings me to that life involves marriage or singleness, sorrow or joy, so be it. Meanwhile there is good advice here for those who are always wondering if some change of personal circumstances or religious discipline would solve all their spiritual problems – it won't!

Chapter 8

'Don't Seek a Wife'!

1 Corinthians 7:25-35

²⁵Now concerning the virgins, I do not have a command of the Lord, but I give an opinion as one who having received the Lord's mercy is trustworthy. ²⁶Therefore I reckon this to be good, that, because of the present distress, it is good for a man to remain as he is. ²⁷Are you attached to a woman? Do not seek to be loosed. Are you free from a woman? Do not seek a woman. ²⁸But if you marry, you do not sin, and if a virgin marries, she does not sin. However, those who do so will have sufferings in the flesh, and I wish to spare you this.

²⁹Therefore I say this, brethren, the time is shortened. For the remainder, therefore, let those who have wives be as those who do not, ³⁰and those who weep as those who do not weep, and those who rejoice as those who do not rejoice, and those who buy as those who possess nothing, ³¹and those who use the world's things as not making full use of them, for the form of this world is passing away.

³²I wish you to be free from concern. The unmarried man is concerned about the things of the Lord, how he might please the Lord. ³³But the married man is concerned about the things of the world, how he might please his wife, ³⁴and he is divided. And the woman who is unmarried and a virgin is concerned about the things of the Lord, how she might be holy both in body and in spirit. But the married woman is concerned about the things of the world, how she might please her husband. ³⁵But this I say to you for your own profit – not that I might cast a restriction around you but for the proper and devoted service of the Lord without distraction.

THE PRESENT DISTRESS

Here Paul finally turns his attention to the single – those who have never married. He refers to them as 'the virgins', which we take from the context to refer both to men and women (though in v.34, as in modern English, it is particularly used of women). As with the case of people married to unbelievers, Paul has no word of Jesus to quote but gives his opinion as one who by the mercy of that same Jesus is 'trustworthy'. Building on the preceding verses, Paul points out that far from solving all our problems marriage brings problems of its own.

This is a reminder which people concerned about marriage do

well to hear. One of the most pernicious phrases in the English language is 'And they all lived happily ever after'. From the nursery onwards it suggests to us there is a stage in this life, usually following marriage, after which we can live in undisturbed bliss. By contrast, Paul describes the time in which he is writing as 'the present distress'. Some suggest that this refers to particular persecution going on in Corinth but there is no indication of this in the letter. Rather the reverse is true – the Corinthians seem to be having an easy time of it (4:8, cf. 4:9-13). It is more likely that Paul refers to the whole of the time before Christ's return. His attitude is that expressed in one famous hymn:

> The world is very evil,
> The hour is waxing late ...

However, it has to be said that this attitude is foreign to most Western Christians. We have grown accustomed to the idea that life in general and the Christian life in particular can be one of growing security and prosperity. Of course, security and prosperity are part of the blessings God promises to his people in the Bible. But, like the Corinthians, we have forgotten that these promises apply to the time *after* Christ's return. So we pray for peace and we look forward to sitting comfortably under our particular 'fig tree' (Micah 4:4) without considering that true peace, both internationally and individually, will only come when Christ finally returns to reign (cf. Micah 4:3). The New Testament tells us that until that time, the world will go on the way it always has and that Christians will frequently suffer hardship. We tend to think that the 'normal' Christian life consists of a happy childhood, a dream wedding, a successful career and a cosy retirement, and there are plenty of churches where either the teaching (quite falsely) promises these things or where the social background of the congregation leads people to expect them. Of course, these things are to be appreciated, and some people actually experience them. But we need to realize that such an experience is *abnormal*. For most people, life is pretty tough, and for most Christians it is even tougher because, on top of the usual problems, they have the particular problems that come from being a Christian.

During the writing of this book I attended a baptism at an Iranian-speaking church. The congregation were generally prosperous and optimistic people typical of their part of North West London, but the service took place the week after two prominent Christians in Iran had been murdered for their faith. These men had friends in the church and news of their deaths brought a passion to the baptism service which is often missing in less troubled, though equally prosperous, circles. We are fortunate in the UK to be able to think of marriage, career and retirement as opportunities for Christians to enjoy. In Iran and other Islamic countries these opportunities are best available to Christians if they become Muslims. To remain a Christian is to court discrimination and even death. The married person in such a situation faces greater strains and anxieties than the single, and this is part of what Paul means by 'sufferings in the flesh' (v.28). Paul's advice is that we should 'sit light' to the things of the world. The married should live as if unmarried, those with many possessions as if they possessed nothing, and so on, by recognizing that these are temporary blessings which cannot be the source of our final security. Martin Luther expressed this attitude in his hymn *Ein' Feste Burg (A Safe Stronghold)*:

> And though they take our life,
> > goods, honour, children, wife,
> > yet is their profit small;
> > > **these things shall vanish all:**
> > the City of God remaineth.

It is, of course, an easier attitude to adopt if you have no wife, children or goods in the first place. However, the point Paul is making is not that we should *never* marry, but that *we should not set our sights on marriage*. His advice parallels that given by Jesus in Matthew 6:31-33!

'Therefore do not be anxious, saying, "What shall we eat?" or "What shall we drink?" or "What shall we wear?" For the Gentiles seek all these things; and your heavenly Father knows that you need them all. But seek first his kingdom and his righteousness, and all these things shall be yours as well.' (RSV)

On the principle that morally neutral circumstances are no hindrance to Christian living, the man who is 'attached to a woman' should not seek to break off this relationship. (Speaking as he is to 'virgins', Paul probably means someone who is *engaged* rather than married - see Fee, pp. 331- 332.) Nor should those who are unattached seek marriage (though, of course, if either marries it is not a sin, as Paul hastens to point out). What we should all seek instead is the Kingdom of God and let other things follow on from that. If, in seeking the 'Kingdom of God', we find we have not had an opportunity to marry, we may be sure that this was for good reasons. Equally, if in the same process we find marriage coming our way we may be sure that this, too, is good and is God's will for us.

THE ANXIETIES OF MARRIAGE

But Paul also counsels against marriage because *marriage itself* brings problems which single people need to think about. Archbishop Geoffrey Fisher apparently said, 'A woman is a great help to a man in all the problems a bachelor never has' – and there is a certain wisdom here. The Bible is quite clear that the first duty of Christians in terms of good works is towards their families. 1 Timothy 5:8 says, 'If any one does not provide for his relatives, and especially for his own family, he has disowned the faith and is worse than an unbeliever.' Clearly, the closer the family member, the greater the duty. So Paul says that the married man or woman cannot simply serve the Lord 'without distraction'. They are concerned with pleasing the Lord, but they are also *quite properly* concerned with pleasing their wife or husband. Significantly, Paul does *not* say that married people should spend less time on their families. That would be to undermine one of the key pillars of church life. Many church families, particularly those of full-time ministers, see too little of one another because of their church activities. But the unmarried simply do not have this problem.

I'M SORRY TO LEAVE YOU FOR THE WEEKEND AGAIN - BUT IT'S ESSENTIAL I ATTEND THIS CONFERENCE ON THE BREAKDOWN OF FAMILY LIFE!!

Marriage brings other anxieties and even sorrows. Family members have accidents or fall ill, children require constant attention and the cost of living goes up with each new mouth to feed. Again, how many Christians thinking of marriage consider what they would do if, as is quite possible, one of their children were to be born mentally or physically handicapped? And of course *no one* lives 'happily ever after' – death *always* intervenes bringing the greatest sorrow of all. Perhaps the most important question, if you are thinking about marriage, is to ask whether *this* person is one with whom you would be wise to face these difficulties. This is the kind of serious consideration Paul calls us to as we weigh the advantages and disadvantages of singleness.

ESTEEMING SINGLENESS

Unfortunately, although 'family services' have done much to establish the idea that children are as much part of God's people as adults (well, almost – the Baptists still won't baptize them and the Anglicans won't give them communion) they have tended to over-emphasize family life at the expense of those who don't fit the pattern. Moreover, evangelical churches show a strong preference for married ministers over against the single. I am never sure whether this is because they like the married 'image', because they think of a wife as a free curate, or because they are afraid single men might be 'gay'. Whatever the reason, it clearly ignores the teaching of the Bible. Of course, ministers should be *free* to marry, but for sheer 'value for money' the single are to be preferred! There is a serious need for our churches to esteem singleness as highly as the Bible does.

Ultimately, however, it is our *freedom* to marry or not which Paul emphasises time and again. In v.28 he says that single people who marry do not sin and in v.35 he concludes by saying that he is not trying to restrict the Corinthians. His only concern is to establish the point that singleness brings opportunities for undivided service which marriage takes away. As such, we should regard singleness (whether short or long term) as an available option and, since we all start out single, we should approach life from the point of view of seeking the Kingdom of God, not the end of our singleness, as our priority.

Chapter 9

Whom Should I Marry, and When?

1 Corinthians 7:36-40

[36]If anyone reckons himself to be acting shamefully towards his virgin, if things are going too far and so it ought to be, let him do what he wishes – he does not sin – let them marry. [37]But he who is established firmly in his heart, not having any necessity, but has authority over his own will, and who has decided this in his own heart: to keep her as his own virgin – he will do well. [38]So then both he who marries his own virgin does well, and he who does not marry her will do even better.

[39]A woman is bound for as long a time as her husband lives. But if the husband falls asleep, she is free to marry whom she wishes, only in the Lord. [40]But she is more blessed if she remains as she is, according to my own opinion, and I consider that I, too, have the Spirit of God.

THE ULTIMATE QUESTION

For many Christians the 'Ultimate Question' is 'How will I know whom to marry and when to marry them?' Regarding almost any other choice they may be willing to accept that you could work it out for yourself without doing too much damage, but when it comes to 'marriage guidance' they are convinced something special is called for. And to some extent they are correct – marriage is a lifelong commitment with serious implications. As the Anglican *Alternative Service Book* says, 'it must not be undertaken carelessly, lightly, or selfishly, but reverently, responsibly, and after serious thought'. We should certainly try to get it right, but making the final choice may be easier than most people imagine!

Here are some bad reasons for choosing to marry:

I might not get a better chance	But then again you might.
I might get left on the shelf	Better the shelf than the divorce courts.

I'm desperate.	You'd marry someone you chose when you were desperate?
I want to get away from home	So move.
All my friends are doing it	No reason why *you* should.
We're in love	So was Amnon with Tamar (2 Sam 13:1-29).
Everyone says we are right for one another	They're not the ones getting married.
God says we are right for one another.	Oh yeah?

Actually the last reason is quite a good one. The problem is, how do you know whether God has said this or not? I well remember some Christian friends of mine telling me about the Bible verse that 'confirmed' they should marry. Their engagement later broke up. Knowing how God tells you whom and when to marry is what this chapter is about.

BE SPECIFIC

The first question to ask is, 'Whom have I in mind?' If you don't have someone specific in mind there is no point worrying about whether to marry. You would be literally worrying over nothing. You don't know whether God will grant you a long life or a short one. You don't know whether a marriage partner will come along in your teens or your sixties. Until there is someone specific in mind, the only realistic question is, 'What *sort* of person should I marry?'

Regarding this question, the Bible lays down some basic requirements which are developed from Genesis 2 onwards. It must be someone who is free to marry (we have seen that Jesus had strong things to say about adultery and 'divorces of convenience'). It must be someone of the opposite sex (marriage is about a man and a woman becoming 'one flesh'). It must be someone to whom you are not too closely related (certain prohibitions are contained in Leviticus 18:6-18 and in the modern laws of many countries) and it must be another Christian (what Paul means by 'in the Lord', v.39). If the person you have in mind fails on one of these points then unfortunately you have to recognize *this is not a person God would want you to marry*. This may sound harsh now and it may involve some difficult choices, but it calls for growth in love and obedience towards God.

MARRY WHOM YOU LIKE!
Apart from that, however, the Bible says *you can marry anyone you like*! In v.39 Paul writes, 'A woman is bound for as long a time as her husband lives. But if the husband falls asleep, she is free to marry *whom she wishes*'. (Feminists please note, in the Bible women *do* have a choice.) This idea comes as a shock to a lot of people, especially those who believe that marriages are 'made in Heaven'. 'Surely', they say, 'God has a plan for my life and there is only one special person whom I should marry?' And from one perspective this is true. God *is* Sovereign, and he *does* have a plan for your life. (Though remember what was said above – God's plan may be that you should only live a short while, or that you should remain single.) But *you* still have to make the choice and, within the limits set out above, marrying someone you *want* to marry is not a bad idea!

Those who are convinced God will tell them whom to marry have generally not considered *how* he will do this. Usually they think they will 'just know'. But this is actually a dangerous way to choose because it not only ignores what the Bible says and focuses on our feelings, but it focuses on the *wrong* feelings. Instead of our feelings about our potential partner we focus on our feelings about what God is 'saying'. Yet if we considered what God *has said* in the Bible we would pay more attention to our feelings about our partner and less to our feelings about what God *might* be saying. When we turn to the Bible we find God speaks to us in two ways –

generally, in the form of Wisdom, and *specifically* in the form of instructions about Christian living.

THE BIBLE AND WISDOM

The 'Wisdom' literature of the Bible (Proverbs, Ecclesiastes, etc.) is usually neglected by Christians because they don't know what to do with it. This is a shame because when read through New Testament eyes it gives profound insight into the issues of daily living.[17] On the subject of marriage it tells us two things are important: *friendship* and *sex*.

The book of Proverbs tells us many things about the qualities of a 'good wife' and the atmosphere of a happy home. Proverbs 31:10-31 is famous for its description of a married woman who is a 'domestic engineer' *par excellence*, running her household and a small business on the side. Not all of us can find someone (or be ourselves) so industrious, but the lessons of Proverbs are clear. Our first question about a potential marriage partner should be, 'Is this someone with whom it would be *wise* to choose to share the rest of my life?'

But you can share your home and your life with a whole lot of people, including those of the same sex – you don't necessarily want to *marry* them! Marriage is more than a *domestic convenience*, it is an *erotic relationship*. If you are obedient to God, marriage is the only context for a sexual relationship you will ever have. We marry – we enter into a lifelong covenant for better for worse, for richer for poorer – because *this* person is special in a way that goes beyond friendship to a love that has a special intensity. In the Wisdom literature the Song of Songs is the supreme expression of this:

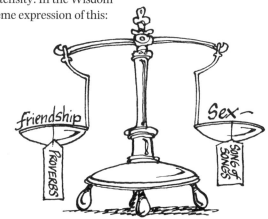

'Set me as a seal upon your heart,
    as a seal upon your arm;
for love is strong as death,
    jealousy is cruel as the grave.
Its flashes are flashes of fire,
    a most vehement flame.
Many waters cannot quench love,
    neither can floods drown it.
If a man offered for love
    all the wealth of his house,
it would be utterly scorned.'
(8:6-7, RSV)

The Bible *does* understand the concept of 'being in love' - and physical attraction is a vital part of it. Looks aren't everything, but they are *something*, as many passages of the Song of Songs testify. Where Proverbs is pragmatic, the Song of Songs is passionate. Proverbs talks about domestic life, budgets and children. The Song of Songs talks of lips and breasts, hair and teeth. But because physical attraction can be felt for a whole range of people we are *wise* to consider the pragmatic qualities first and the physical qualities second. We should enjoy the *person* as much as we enjoy his or her *body*. As Proverbs 31:30 points out:

> 'Charm is deceitful, and beauty is vain,
>   but a woman [or, we might add, a man] who fears the Lord
>   is to be praised.' (RSV)

Even in the Song of Songs, *friendship* is a vital ingredient of true love:

> 'This is my beloved and this is my friend,
>   O daughters of Jerusalem.' (5:16, RSV)

Wisdom will not tell us specifically whom to marry, but it will allow us to narrow the field. It enables us to move from asking, 'Is this someone I would like to marry?' through, 'Is this someone I would be *wise* to marry?' to, 'Is this someone I would *love* to marry?' If the answer to all three is 'Yes' you are on the right track!

IS THIS 'IT' ?
So here you are. You are a Christian with another Christian in mind who is not disqualified as a marriage partner. You value one another's personal qualities, you are physically attracted to one another and you are true friends. You are, in fact, 'in love'. But is this enough? How do you know whether to marry or not? The answer the Bible gives in 1 Corinthians 7 is, 'If you must marry, *do*. If you needn't marry, *don't*.' The key to knowing the difference is *sex*.

Paul advises single people facing the choice of marriage as follows:

'If anyone reckons himself to be acting shamefully towards his virgin, if things are going too far, and so it ought to be, let him do what he wishes – he does not sin – let them marry.'

Once again, however, there are two important questions of interpretation here: to whom is Paul talking and what does he mean?

WHOSE VIRGIN?

Some people have suggested that Paul is not talking to couples at all, but to a father about his daughter whom he is holding back from marriage. The NASB translation is based on this assumption, but it raises several problems. One is that, if this is what Paul is saying, he praises the father, not the daughter, for her remaining single:

'So then both **he** who gives his own virgin daughter in marriage **does well**, and **he** who does not give her in marriage **will do even better**. (NASB)

Whilst a key argument of 1 Corinthians 7 is that 'singleness is good for the single', it is hard to see how a daughter's singleness could be good for her *father*. It is even harder to see how this would be so if she were kept single without regard for her wishes, which is implied by this interpretation. It might be held that Paul means the father would do better *for his daughter*, but this does not agree with the flow of the chapter. Paul has constantly emphasised that marriage is a *good* option for those who choose it. Even his strongest argument for remaining single is not designed to constrain this choice (v.35). It is hardly likely he would then encourage a father to override his daughter's desires and keep her single.

But the main problem is that this interpretation rests entirely on a single change of verb – from one meaning 'to marry' in v.36 to one meaning 'to give in marriage' in v.38. *Apart from this we would naturally assume Paul is talking to couples.* Whilst we must admit it is hard to see why Paul made the change, it is even harder to believe that it means he is talking about fathers and daughters. We therefore conclude that the more obvious meaning is correct – Paul is talking to what we would call 'engaged' couples. But what is he saying?

WHAT IS 'TOO FAR'?

Whomever Paul is talking to, he says they should marry 'if things are going too far'. Some translations take this as a reference to the woman's age – 'if she is getting past it'. But this conjures up the unlikely image of ageing virgins wondering whether to go ahead and marry or not. In a congregation only four years old, one doubts whether there would have been time for this to become a common problem! The phrase Paul uses is enticingly – we might say deliberately – vague. It consists of only two Greek words, *ei huperakmos*, which could be translated 'If he, or she, or it, is "over the top"' (literally, 'past the acme'). But this phrase follows Paul's earlier reference to the man 'acting shamefully', which is much clearer. Elsewhere in 1 Corinthians (12:23) the same root word refers to the parts of the body we keep covered up ('our *indecorous* parts'). In Romans 1:27 it refers to indecent homosexual practices and in Revelation 16:15 it refers to shameful nakedness. Clearly 'going too far' has something to do with *sexual* shame and it is fairly easy to imagine to what Paul is referring. This is not a case of a Christian father being commended for holding back his daughter from marriage but of a Christian couple being rebuked for 'going too far' in their sexual behaviour before marriage.

PAUL'S SOLUTION

However, there is a striking contrast between Paul's solution to this problem and the advice we tend to give in similar situations. We urge people to exercise more self-control, to draw the line at certain behaviours, to take more time to get to know one another and so on. Paul's solution is more simple. As in the case of widowers and widows he declares, 'Let them marry!'

It would be worth trying this next time you hear of a couple – maybe friends of yours or perhaps in your church youth group – who complain about the difficulties of sexual self-control. Tell them to get married. Their answers will reveal a lot about their thinking. Most people have a barrage of reasons why this would be impossible:

- We haven't had enough time to get to know one another yet.
- We're not sure if we're sexually compatible.
- We're not ready for marriage.
- We aren't old enough.

- We can't afford it.
- We're saving up.
- Our parents wouldn't approve.
- We're engaged – we're getting married next year.

The rebuke the Bible gives to all these reasons is the same, '**If you're not ready for marriage *to* one another, you're not ready for sex *with* one another.**' In the Bible sex without a marriage covenant is fornication.

But how can Paul be so confident that the couples concerned are ready for marriage? The answer is that if they have approached the *rest* of their relationship Christianly then the raising of the sexual temperature is a good indication that it is time to get married. Naturally, we don't have to be like the Corinthians and wait until our behaviour is shameful. **The time to marry is when sex becomes an issue but before it becomes a problem.**

NO SEX, PLEASE, WE'RE SINGLE

Of course, if you really aren't ready for marriage because you don't know one another well enough, or you are too young, or there is some other good reason, then you *shouldn't* marry. But if this is the case, you shouldn't be involved with one another sexually either.

If sexual attraction is God's way of telling us when and whom to marry then *we should avoid arousing sexual passions with someone we have no intention of marrying*. Unfortunately, Christians today have accepted the idea that sexual activity and 'dating' go together. We have developed a 'Richter Scale' of what is permitted and what isn't – genital intercourse is wrong, but passionate kisses are generally OK, physical caresses are for couples who really like one another, and if you are engaged you can go almost the whole way! Somewhere between kissing and orgasm we try to draw a 'Christian' line – but this is all Pharisaism. People who ask 'How far can we go?' are not looking for a limit but an excuse. The question for a Christian should not be 'How far can I go?' but 'How can I remain holy?' *Until marriage is in prospect there is really no reason why you should 'go' anywhere.* This may sound legalistic, but it is actually *realistic*. With sex one thing leads to another – God designed it that way. Within marriage it leads ultimately to

the joyful consummation of becoming 'one flesh'. Outside marriage it leads to a devaluing of the deed and of the relationships that go with it.

Another reason for avoiding sexual activity in courtship, and one that is often overlooked, is that sex is a process by which the two become 'one flesh'. This happens whether we are aware of it or not and whether we intend it to or not. In 1 Cor 6 Paul says that we can even become one flesh with a prostitute (v.16). Sexual involvement with a person leads to an involvement of the whole person – that is what it is designed to do. For this reason, the breaking of a close relationship which has had a sexual component is particularly painful. There is a tearing apart of the 'one flesh' – and the greater the sexual component, the greater the pain. Controlling your own inclinations and *refusing* the advances of another is therefore both wise and loving, especially if you explain why.

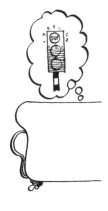

There is also a common sense reason for abstaining from sexual activity in courtship which has nothing to do with selfish motives like avoiding AIDS. Quite simply, it is difficult to get to know someone as a person when you are involved with them sexually. It is hard to tell whether it is the person you like or just the sex. (It could, of course, be both but it is still hard to tell.) The Song of Songs contains a refrain which says:

'I adjure you, O daughters of Jerusalem,
that you stir not up nor awaken love
until it please.' (8:4, also 2:7; 3:5, RSV)

Interpretations of this vary, but I suspect it has something to do
with not arousing passions which cannot be fulfilled (cf. 4:16). It
is wise to avoid responding to any sexual attraction until you
have had plenty of time to get to know one another as people. In
marriage you are going to spend far more time talking to one
another than having sex with one another and this should be
reflected in your courtship.

This does not mean that all physical contact before marriage is
wrong, but there is a clear difference between affectionate and
arousing behaviour.[18] Holding hands, hugging and the occasional
kiss are fine, but long sessions on the sofa are a mistake. Of course,
feeling sexual passion is not wrong. Even giving in to it would not
be the end of the world – nor, if you do so, does it mean that you
must marry. But it should be seen as an indication either that
marriage should be in view or that this relationship has taken a
wrong turning. When, after spending time getting to know one
another, there is clearly a mutual sexual attraction between two
people it is time to start planning for marriage. If sexual attraction
is treated with respect it will help you to understand the nature of
your relationship and to be confident of the timing of your
marriage when and if it takes place. If it is just a 'green light' for
personal indulgence it may lead to actions you regret, and to
heartache and unforseen problems for the future.

TRY BEFORE YOU BUY?

There is a school of thought which suggests that sexual activity
during courtship, or even a period of 'living together', is a vital
test of sexual compatibility in marriage. In response, it first needs
to be said that there is no such thing as a 'trial marriage'. You
cannot have a *temporary* permanent relationship. Enjoying – or
even not enjoying – sex when you are unmarried is not an
absolute guide to what it will be like when you are married. But
second, if one of you is male and the other female you are already
a long way towards compatibility. If, in addition to this, you are
both attracted to one another enough to want to try having sex
then it is hard to see what the worry is. 'Sexual compatibility' is

not something which a couple either have or don't have. Learning to please one another sexually takes time, love and, above all, communication. If you want to ensure sexual compatibility, start by practising verbal and emotional compatibility.

CHRISTIAN ENGAGEMENTS

A truly Christian courtship would thus look very odd in the world's eyes. There would be a long period when nothing much seemed to be happening – when people weren't even sure if a couple were an 'item'. Then there would be the sudden announcement of a marriage only a few weeks away. The reason for this short engagement, however, would not be because the bride was pregnant but because the couple were sure of their feelings and wanted to *avoid* sexual sin.

The fly in the ointment is, of course, the wedding arrangements. Weddings were originally designed to make a public declaration of a marriage covenant and to give family and friends a chance to celebrate. The modern wedding is an invention of the 'wedding industry' and is often a financial and emotional burden on a couple which, by delaying the marriage itself, causes many of them to sin sexually. Significantly, the Bible has a lot to say about sex and marriage but has almost nothing to say about weddings. It doesn't even say who should 'conduct' them and we must conclude that they really don't matter that much. It actually takes less than a month to organize the legal aspects of a wedding and very few people fill up their diaries (if they have them) much more than six weeks in advance. If strong sexual desire is already part of a mature relationship then three or four months is probably quite long enough to have to suppress it. You really *don't* have to spend a fortune on clothes, flowers, food, video photographers and so on. If you must invite Uncle Tom Cobbleigh and all to your wedding, you could arrange the ceremony, hire a hall and get family and friends to provide a buffet in a fraction of the time and at a fraction of the cost usually involved. If people want to spend more money on you, let them buy some of the things for your home which you can't afford yourselves.

Some people say that the engagement serves another function, by allowing people time in which to change their minds about marriage. But this is a quite dangerous suggestion. It means that people will indeed get engaged when they are not absolutely sure about marriage, imagining they can back out later. However, the next stage is planning the wedding and once this is under way *it is very difficult indeed to get off the conveyor belt*. When premises and businesses have been booked and people invited, it is very hard to say 'No' even when your mind is full of doubts. On the contrary, the pressure to go ahead is almost impossible to resist. I really dread to think how many people get married, having become engaged from a position of uncertainty, because they just can't bear to stop the 'marriage machine'. If you are not ready for marriage *now* you are not ready to get engaged. And if you are ready now why make the engagement longer than necessary?

Martin Luther, the great reformer, decided to marry Katherine von Bora in May 1525. He was engaged on the 13th June and celebrated the marriage on the 27th. Writing on the subject of long engagements, he said:

> 'Scripture, experience, and all creation testify that the gifts of God must be taken on the wing.' [19]

WHEN TO WAIT

Of course, you don't *have* to get married – the choice is there not to. In v.38, Paul indicates the kind of couple who definitely should wait in contrast to the couple who should marry. He emphasises four times that the decision to remain unmarried must be based on the relationship being entirely under control:

> 'But he who is (1) established firmly in his heart, (2) not having any necessity, but (3) has authority over his own will, and who (4) has decided this in his own heart: to keep her as his own virgin – he will do well.'

However, if sexual self-control is not an issue in a relationship then the couple don't need to marry *and therefore normally they shouldn't*.[20] Marriage is usually a once-in-a-lifetime decision. It is certainly a lifelong commitment. It brings anxieties and problems of its own and it takes away opportunities for Christian service. Why choose to marry a particular person when there is no compelling reason? You have all the advantages of singleness, none of the problems of marriage, and all the joys of friendship. Why spoil it?

Paul's final comment to both couples reinforces this point:

'So then both he who marries his own virgin does well, and he who does not marry her will do even better.'

Marriage is good and singleness is good, but in the present life singleness has an extra quality of good, since it keeps us from particular anxieties and frees us for Christian service. If in doubt, you can be sure that to marry will eventually bring those anxieties, but to go on being single certainly won't.

NO GUARANTEES!

The guidance the Bible gives is that the person you should marry is a friend who would be a *wise* choice and a lover who would be a *compelling* choice. The time to marry is *after* the friendship has been proved and *before* sexual attraction becomes a problem. Following this guidance will not guarantee a happy marriage – it remains for better for worse, for richer for poorer, in sickness and in health – but it will be a marriage where you can be sure your decisions were, to the best of your ability, wise and Godly. Taken in conjunction with the rest of 1 Corinthians 7 and the Bible as a whole, you will certainly avoid many of the traps and pitfalls which lead people into unsuitable marriages at present.

Chapter 10

Concluding Postscript

1 Corinthians 7:39-40

[39]A woman is bound for as long a time as her husband lives. But if the husband falls asleep, she is free to marry whom she wishes, only in the Lord. [40]But she is more blessed if she remains as she is, according to my own opinion, and I consider that I, too, have the Spirit of God.

I have long been struck by the fact that the last two verses of 1 Corinthians 7 seem to be both repetitive and personal. Paul has spoken to widows before (vv.8-9) and has also made it quite clear that marriage is for life (vv.10-11). Going over the same ground here suggests to me it is a 'PS' addressed to a specific person with a specific problem. And this is a good reminder with which to finish. This book talks about general principles, but in the end they have to be applied by individual people in their own situations. I always picture the woman Paul is addressing as having a sickly husband whom she no longer really loves and a secret admiration for someone in the congregation whom she would like to marry – though this may be my overactive imagination! But there will be people reading this book whose lives may be directly affected by what I have said. This is an awesome prospect and a reminder to us Bible teachers of the seriousness of our responsibility.

In the end it is you, the individual, with whom God is dealing, and you who must deal with God and the people in your life. There are *general* principles, but there is only *individual* application. Read not only this book but the Bible, and not only 1 Corinthians 7 but the whole of Scripture. Pray about it and think about it. Ultimately we must seek holiness rather than fulfilment, and the Kingdom of God rather than singleness or marriage:

'For the Gentiles seek all these things; and your heavenly Father knows that you need them all. But seek first his kingdom and his righteousness, and all these things shall be yours as well.' (Matthew 6:32-33, RSV)

Endnotes

1. Augustine of Hippo, **Confessions**, Tr. Henry Chadwick (Oxford: Oxford University Press, 1992), pp.150-153

2. Ibid. p.145

3. R.J. Foster **Money, Sex and Power** (London: Hodder and Stoughton, 1985) p.101

4. Quoted in R.H. Bainton **Sex, Love and Marriage: A Christian Survey** (London: Fontana, 1957) p.32

5. Plato **The Republic**, Tr. H.D.P. Lee (Harmondsworth: Penguin, 1974) p.444, emphasis added

6. Augustine of Hippo, **Confessions and Enchiridion**, Tr. Albert C. Outler, (London: SCM, 1955)

7. Of course, if you still think that in vv.1-6 Paul is advising single Christians to marry in order to avoid sexual temptation you have an even bigger problem since here he is saying he would much rather they remained single. Surely, as we have argued, it is easier to assume that the first paragraph is addressed to married couples?

8. C.H. Talbert, **Reading Corinthians** (New York: Crossroads Publishing Company, 1987) p.39

9. P. Jensen & A. Payne, **The Last Word on Guidance** (Kingswood: ANZEA/St. Matthias Press, 1991) p.138

10. P. Bolt, **Sex and the Single?** The Briefing, No.62, Feb. 1991, p.6

11. Jensen & Payne, **op. cit.** p.140, emphasis added.

12. Ibid. p.141

13. Jesus' comment about 'the angels' here is not a comment about gender so much as a dig at the Sadducees who didn't believe in angels or the resurrection.

14. It is just possible, but unlikely given the flow of the argument, that Paul means the Christian might indeed save the unbelieving husband or wife if he or she stays. However, the advice to let a deserting partner go still stands.

15. It is important to understand that the biblical concept of 'calling' does not refer to career but to conversion – we all share one calling, to become Christians and live a holy life.

16. It is sometimes argued that Paul meant that if the opportunity for freedom came along the slave should refuse it and 'use' his slavery instead, but this is so unlikely on linguistic, contextual, historical and common sense grounds I think we are safe in rejecting it (see Fee, pp.316-318).

17. See G. Goldsworthy, **Gospel and Wisdom** (Exeter, Paternoster Press, 1987)

18. See E. Vaughan & A. Stewart, **Starting Out: First Steps in the Christian Life** (London: St. Matthias Press, 1993) for some wise words in this respect.

19. Quoted in R.H. Bainton, **Here I Stand** (Oxford: Lion Publishing, 1978), p.289

20. An exception might be, for example, a much older couple who marry primarily out of love and friendship, but exceptions 'prove the rule'.

Study Guide

This study guide is designed for use by individuals, couples and groups. In churches it may be particularly useful in marriage preparation and in youth work. The study guide roughly follows the order of the chapters of *God, Sex & Marriage* so that you can work through it as you read the book. However, it assumes people will read the book as a whole, not just the parts related to the studies. It also brings in additional biblical material, not covered in *God, Sex & Marriage*, which raises new questions and suggests new avenues to explore.

There are six studies in all. Some of them will take longer than others and may need to run over more than one session. Each study has a brief introduction and a series of questions, some for everyone to discuss, others particularly for couples to consider. However, this is not a rigid rule—you can tackle any question you find interesting! The questions should be used as a starting point, not the last word on the subject. By all means ask your own questions, but make sure that you read the Bible passages suggested.

Study 1

Let's talk about sex!

Read the 'Introduction', pp 9-11
Christian preachers often give the ancient city of Corinth a worse reputation than it deserves. Old Corinth was lampooned for its sexual immorality by Greek playwrights, but this city was flattened in the wars with the Romans in 146 BC and then rebuilt as a colony about a century later. The Corinth Paul visited in 50 AD was a multi-cultural metropolis, probably no better or worse than any other commercial sea port of its day.[1]

However, we all tend to learn about sex from the culture around us, and this certainly seems to have been true of the Christians in the church at Corinth. Some of them were very 'libertarian' - taking an 'anything goes' view. Others were very strict - seeing sex as 'dangerous and dirty'. What neither group had was a truly biblical view.

For Everyone
1. How and where did you learn about sex?

2. Was the information factually accurate?

3. What did you learn then about the morality of sex? Did it make you think that sex was:
(a) 'OK with anybody, so long as you're loving and careful',
(b) 'Not really a "nice" thing to do' or
(c) something else (if so, what)?

4. What are your current views about sexual morality and why do you hold them?

For Couples
5. Following on from question 4, do you both share the same views about sexual morality? Does this matter to you?

---

1 C K Barrett, Black's New Testament Commentaries: The First Epistle to the Corinthians - Second Edition (London: A & C Black, 1971) pp 1-3

For Everyone
Read 'Sex and Spirituality', pp 18-20
6. Do you think Christians are positive or negative about sex?
What gives you this impression?

7. Does 'sexiness' go with godliness, or do you think the two are
really incompatible? Why do you hold this opinion?

Read 1 Timothy 4:1-5
8. What else does this passage tell us about Paul's attitude to sex
and marriage?

Read the Song of Songs 4:1-5:1 and Proverbs 31:10-31
9. How do these two passages differ in their understanding of a
'good relationship'? What does this teach us about assessing our
own relationships?

10. Does it matter if a couple don't feel 'madly in love' all the time?
How can they cope with their changing feelings?

Study 2

Not Tonight Dear?

Read 'Sex in Marriage', pp 20-23
A major cause of strain in relationships is the different attitudes men and women have to sex. Not for nothing do we talk about the 'opposite' sex! The emphasis in the Bible is that in marriage husbands and wives give up their 'rights' to their own bodies and instead take on the duty - and pleasure - of serving one another (1 Corinthians 7:3-5). But this means learning about and focussing on what pleases the other person, which takes time, effort and love.

For everyone

1. How do you feel about surrendering your rights over your own body and using it to serve someone else?

2. How does this make you feel about your body? How does it make you feel about a prospective partner

For couples

Read the 'Summary', p 23
3. How can you help your partner avoid the temptation of wrong sexual or emotional relationships? What should you do when one of you isn't in the mood for sex and the other is?

For everyone

Read 'Thinking it Through', pp 23-27
4. What do you understand by the expression 'other-centred sexuality' (p 24)? Does this idea encourage or irritate you?

Read 1 Timothy 2:9-10 and the Song of Songs 7:1-6
5. How can we hold these two passages in balance?

6. Write down what you think makes someone attractive to the opposite sex. Share and discuss your opinions with someone of the opposite sex!

7. What do you think about 'dressing to please'? How can men and women serve one another in the way they dress?

8. How would you find out about the sexual and emotional feelings of the opposite sex? Do you think it is right to do this? Have you ever made any effort to do this?

9. Which of the things that first attract a couple last through a lifetime of marriage? Which things change and how can we adjust to them?

For couples
10. Have you ever wished your partner dressed or acted differently from the way he or she does? Have you ever tried to get him or her to change? What has this done to your partner? What has it done to your relationship?

Study 3

For better, for worse?

Nobody lives 'happily ever after'. Marriage brings tears as well as joy. Even the best marriage ends in death, and sometimes this comes tragically soon. Many people are tempted to divorce and children bring stresses to a relationship as well as having their own problems as they grow up. We need to think seriously about the 'darker' side of marriage. But first we need to see that marriage is one form of what the Bible calls a 'covenant'.

Read Genesis 2:24
This defines the marriage covenant as having three features: leaving to start a new family, cleaving by committing yourself to someone else, and uniting with that person through sexual intercourse.

Read Exodus 20:14
'Adultery' means 'breaking the marriage covenant by wrongful sexual intercourse'.

For everyone
1. Why does the Bible make such an issue of adultery?

2. How should the knowledge that marriage is for life affect our choice of marriage partner?

3. Why does the Bible's teaching about marriage make it wise for Christians to marry only Christians?

For couples
4. Do you both agree that marriage is for life?

5. What would committing adultery say about your attitude to your spouse? What would it do to your marriage?

For everyone
Read 'Marriage, Divorce and Separation', pp 37-43

6. Why does God hate divorce (p 39-43, Malachi 2:16)? How should Christians treat divorced people?

Read 'Mixed Marriages and Desertion', pp 44-48, Ezra 10:2-3 and Matthew 19:3-9
7. In what way does Paul's advice about mixed marriage (ie between a Christian and a non-Christian, 1 Cor 7:12-16) differ from that given in Ezra? What reason does Paul give which might explain this difference?

8. In what way does Paul's advice to Christians whose non-Christian partners desert them differ from the answer Jesus gives to the Pharisees in Matthew 19? Why is there this difference?

9. In what circumstances, if any, is remarriage possible after divorce or desertion?

10. What support do Christians in mixed marriages need from other Christians?

For couples
11. Should you treat your children (a) as little pagans until they make a definite response to the gospel, (b) as little Christians until they definitely turn away from Christ or (c) something else? Do you agree together on this?

12. What would you do if you found out one of your children might be born deformed or disabled?

13. Have you planned for emergencies by making a will, taking out life insurance, etc.? If not, why not?

For everyone
Read 'God and the Bereaved', pp 35-36
14. How should you treat people who have suffered a family tragedy? Why is this issue so important?

Study 4

Using Your Gift

Read 'Is There a Gift of Singleness?', pp 28-30
The medieval church used to think you were more 'spiritual' if
you remained unmarried. As a result, tens of thousands of men
and women lived their whole lives in monasteries and nunneries.
The Reformation changed all that, but people still get the idea that
God gives some people the special gift of being 'happily single'.

For everyone
Read Matthew 19:8-12
1. Does Jesus suggest you need more of a special gift to be married
or to be single?

2. What is God's solution for someone who is unhappily single or
unhappily married?

3. If you want to get married, but can't find a partner, are you just
being too fussy? If not, why do you think it is that you are still
single?

Read 'What Is He Saying?', pp 32-34
4. How should single and unmarried people deal with sexual
temptation? How can they lessen the risks? How can they
increase their self-control?

5. How can Christians help one another with sexual self-control?

Read 'Be What You Are', pp 49-52
6. How do you see the signs of God's sovereignty (his hand at
work) in your life? To what extent was your becoming a Christian
a result of circumstances beyond your control?

7. Is God still in control of your life when you don't obey him?

8. What do you like and what don't you like about your present
circumstances? In what ways would changing your

circumstances affect your service of God?

9. How could you make your life more positive without changing the things you don't really like?

10. People often say "I could be an effective Christian if only..." What are the common "if onlys"? Are they right?

For couples
11. How should you deal with unhappiness or temptations in your own relationship?

For everyone
Read 'Don't Seek a Wife'!, pp 53-57
12. List the disadvantages of marriage. How would (or do) you cope with these in marriage?

13. If you found yourself becoming attracted to someone, how could you put the Kingdom of God first in developing your relationship with them?

14. Does your church or social group esteem singleness and the single? Why do they take this view? How could they develop and display a more positive view of singleness?

Study 5

... And You Makes Your Choice!

Read 'Whom Should I Marry and When?', pp 58-70
There is no promise in the Bible that God will give us 'special revelation' about whom to marry. God won't point a big finger from the sky at your future marriage partner and say "It's this one!" Instead, the Bible cautions us about the seriousness of marriage (so that we don't rush into it) and advises us to be realistic as well as romantic.

For Everyone
1. If you can't be sure how marriage will work out, how can you ever decide to marry?

Read 2 Samuel 13:1-15
2. What are the dangers of 'romantic love'? In what ways is it an unreliable guide to a choice of marriage partner?

3. What is good about romantic love? Is it completely unnecessary in choosing a marriage partner?

4. How can you tell the difference between true love and infatuation?

Read Proverbs 19:13 and Ephesians 5:22-24
5. What would a wise man look for in a wife? What does a loving wife do for her husband? If you are a woman, are you prepared to do it?

Read Proverbs 5:18-19 and Ephesians 5:25-29
6. What would a wise woman look for in a husband? What does a loving husband do for his wife? If you are a man, are you prepared to do it?

Read the Song of Songs 1:2-4
7. When is kissing a sexual activity? What does it lead to?

8. "If you're not ready for marriage, you're not ready for sex." Discuss!

9. How and when should an unmarried couple show affection? What should they do about any sexual feelings they may have?

10. How can you explore and develop relationships with the opposite sex without necessarily 'dating'?

11. How and why should you put friendship first in a developing relationship? What effect would this have on a subsequent marriage?

For couples
12. If you are planning to marry, how long will you make your engagement? During this time, how will you avoid sexual sin? If you think this will be difficult, why don't you make your engagement shorter?

13. Do you need to marry, or do you just want to marry? If you need to marry, for how long should you put it off?

14. If you don't need to marry, are you really 'just good friends'? Are you enjoying the friendships of others as well?

Study 6

Concluding Postscript

The Bible says you can marry whom you wish, "only in the Lord". This gives us enormous freedom, but also a (perhaps unwelcome) responsibility for our choice of marriage partner.

For everyone
1. What does Paul mean by 'in the Lord' - in other words, what are the essential qualities of a Christian marriage partner (see p 60)? Why are these essential?

2. Apart from these essentials, what restrictions does the Bible place on our choice of marriage partner?

3. What are the qualities men and women would be wise to look for in the opposite sex? What do they actually tend to look for? Why is this so? How can they learn to do better?

4. What do women consider as a 'loving gesture' from a man? What do men consider a 'loving gesture' from a woman? How can single people avoid confusing one another?

5. What are some of the qualities you would regard as optional in a marriage partner?

6. Do you need to become more biblical in your attitude to choosing a marriage partner? If you do, how could you go about making the change?

7. In considering a marriage partner, do you tend to think more about what they could do for you, or do you think more about what you could do for them?

For everyone
8. Throughout this letter, Paul keeps advising people to 'remain as you are'. Why do you think he does this? What should you do when your present circumstances are difficult? When should you change?

9.What does your favourite version of the Bible seem to assume about Paul's views on sex and marriage in 1 Corinthians 7? How does that compare with your own understanding of his views now?

Notes

Study 1

Study 2

Study 3

Study 4

Study 5

Study 6